THE 10 MINUTE COACH

Daily Strategies for Life Success

THE 10 MINUTE COACH

Daily Strategies for Life Success

Dan Lier

BEAUFORT BOOKS   NEW YORK

Library of Congress Cataloging-in-Publication Data

Lier, Dan.
 The 10 minute coach : daily strategies for life success / Dan Lier. — 1st ed.
  p. cm.
 ISBN 0-8253-0543-8 (alk. paper)
 1. Success. 2. Self-help techniques. 3. Self-actualization
(Psychology)
I. Title. II. Title: Ten minute coach.

 BF637.S8L485 2007
 158—dc22
                               2006018643

Published in the United States by Beaufort Books
Distributed by Midpoint Trade Books
www.midpointtrade.com

 2   4   6   8   10 9   7   5   3   1

PRINTED IN THE UNITED STATES OF AMERICA

To all of you who have the burning
desire to be your best; to reach your
true potential; to do something special—
this book is for you.

For those who are or have been confronted
with challenges and obstacles and stare
adversity in the face; your greatest power
is your mindset—your belief about
what you can achieve.

Contents

PART 3
PARENTHOOD AT THE NEXT LEVEL

PART 4
RELATIONSHIPS AT THE NEXT LEVEL

Acknowledgments

First and foremost, I'd like to express my most sincere appreciation to my family for showing me the love and support that made this book possible: to my wife Tammy and our two children, who make my life so special, and to my Dad and Mom for providing me with what I needed to have the unquenchable thirst and drive to achieve. Thank all of you for believing in me and inspiring me every day.

To those who have influenced my growth and career: Tony Robbins, thank you for your leadership and a reference for what's possible with belief and commitment. Brian Tracy, thank you for your late dinner talks about what it takes to be successful and how there are no shortcuts to success. Denis Waitley, thank you for giving me the insight and true understanding about what it takes in commitment and focus to author a book. To my college basketball coach Bill Morse, thank you for testing and conditioning my mental toughness and giving me the reference that overcoming each adversity would bring me one step closer to success. Tom and Amy Kelley, thank you for the major role you played in my life. Peter Boesen, you are a great leader, and thank you for your unwavering belief in me. And thank you, Brett Vice, for your diligence and persistence.

A special thanks to Eric Kampmann at Midpoint Trade books and to David Nelson at Beaufort Books for seeing the vision and making this book possible. Thank you to all the editors, designers, and staff who worked with us to complete this project and make it a success.

Introduction

Welcome to *The 10 Minute Coach.*

My name is Dan Lier. Through my speaking programs, my CD series *The 10 Minute Coach* and *SSP (Subconscious Success Programming)*, and my courses such as High Impact Presentation Skills, I help people all over the world, from CEOs to soccer moms, become their very best. Today I'm excited about having you here with me through this book.

Before we get started, I'd like to salute you for being the type of person who invests in yourself; for taking some time to grab some tools and strategies that will assist you to become your very best. Now the reason I say that is because in my business I meet so many people who are not getting the results they want in their lives, yet are not willing to do anything different. And, of course, that's the definition of insanity: doing the same things over and over and over and expecting something different to happen. So, congratulations! I'm excited to be writing to you, because this book will be a positive force in your life and assist you to reach The Next Level.

I've been professionally speaking, training, and coaching for over a decade, and I've been fortunate enough to work with some of the best of the best in my business: **Brian Tracy, Denis Waitley, Og Mandino**, and **Tony Robbins**. I've seen so many people buy CDs and tapes with the seminars with the intent to apply the information to their lives and their business.

Yet, even when they have the best intentions, our research says that 7 to 13 percent of those people don't even open up the package, and 55 percent never listen to the entire tape or CD series.

At my seminars we started to ask questions. My staff compiled a questionnaire, and our participants simply said the tapes and CDs were too long and it was difficult to stay focused on an entire series. With that information in mind, we created this book as a resource for those committed to be their best. It's been designed to give you short, focused personal coaching sessions on a variety of topics whenever you need them. For instance, if you've had a major disappointment in your life, just go to Chapter 4, "Overcoming Adversity," and you'll get a short, personal coaching session to help you get back on track.

So, whether you just had a major setback and need to turn it around, or maybe you need to create some momentum on a project, or maybe you just need an attitude adjustment, this book will get you there. At the end of each chapter I'm going give you some action steps to take to help you create some momentum and get some positive results. And remember, the more you put into it, the more you get out of it. Use this book as a tool to help you stay focused and on track to take you to The Next Level. So, let's get started!

PART 1

Taking Your Career and Life to the Next Level

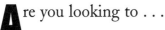

CHAPTER 1

Believing in the Next Level

Are you looking to . . .

- ❏ Make some big changes?
- ❏ Start a new business?
- ❏ Get in the best shape of your life?
- ❏ Or just be your very best?

Whatever you're looking to do, you have to start with the foundation of your success: your *belief system.*

Whenever you meet people who are very successful, people who are very good at what they do, you'll find they have a rock-solid belief system that propels them toward success. Your beliefs are the foundation of your success or your failure.

You see, a belief means a sense of certainty. It's what you're certain about. The people who are most certain about what they're doing are the ones who separate themselves from those who struggle.

THE FIRST FOUR-MINUTE MILE

You may have heard of Roger Bannister, the first man ever to break the four-minute mile in running, back in 1954. Now here's what's interesting about that story. In addition to running, Bannister was studying to be a doctor in England. Back in the 1950s doctors had a belief that no human being would ever break the four-minute mile. There was even an article published in an American medical journal that if a man exerted his body to the level of intensity that it would take to break the four-minute mile, his heart would actually explode inside his body. So, imagine Bannister hanging out with all of his med school colleagues and saying, "Hey, I can do this! I'm eating well. I'm training hard. I can do this!" How do you think they might respond? They'd probably say, "You're nuts! I mean, aren't you reading the journals? Your heart is going to explode!" Not a very compelling future, right?

Well, Bannister went out in 1954 and broke the four-minute mile. Then what do you think happened? The next year, thirty-seven other people broke the four-minute mile, and the year after that, over 200 broke the four-minute mile! Now, of course, even high-school boys turn in four-minute miles on occasion.

So what really changed back in 1954? That's right, it's the belief system. Bannister did what no one else believed could be done, and people said, "Hey, if he can do it, then I can do it!" They changed their beliefs about what was possible for them.

Your beliefs drive your behavior. You cannot get yourself to do something you don't believe is possible. If you don't believe you can be a top sales professional, you won't get yourself to do what's necessary. If you don't believe you can earn a certain dollar amount that you've never earned before, you won't get yourself to follow through and do the things necessary. If you don't believe you can have a successful relationship, than you won't do the things necessary to foster a successful relationship.

BELIEFS THAT HOLD YOU BACK . . . OR DRIVE YOU FORWARD

If I were a single guy (which I'm not), and I saw a woman who was really attractive, I'd be saying to myself, "Man, I want to take her out. I love the way she walks, the way she talks, the hair, the lips, the nails, the whole thing." Yet suppose in my heart I'm saying to myself, "She'll never go out with me. I mean, we probably have nothing in common, she won't find me interesting, she must be already involved with someone else, I won't be able to come up with something to talk about, and if I ask, she'll put me down in front of my friends and everybody." Would I ask her out then? Of course not. You see, beliefs drive your behavior.

Now here's the good news. Who controls what you believe? That's right, you do. Yet maybe you get influenced by the media, the marketplace, interest rates, what happened last year, or what somebody told you. So here's my question to you: *What do you believe?* Is your belief system propelling you to higher heights? Or is it holding you down? Chances are that if you're struggling in this specific area, you have *disempowering* beliefs—beliefs that hold you back.

Let me give you some examples of disempowering beliefs.

- ❒ I'm not good enough.
- ❒ I'm not smart enough.
- ❒ I'm too tall.
- ❒ I'm too short.
- ❒ I didn't go to college.
- ❒ I'm not a good speaker.
- ❒ No one in my family's ever done anything like that.

On the other hand, let me give you some *empowering* beliefs; beliefs that propel you to new heights. Here are a couple of examples:

- ❒ I can do anything I commit to.
- ❒ I'm a great leader.
- ❒ I'm a great sales professional.
- ❒ I earn as much money as I want to earn.
- ❒ I earn $250,000.00.
- ❒ I earn half a million dollars.
- ❒ I'm an amazing parent.
- ❒ People love to be around me.

TRUTH AND BELIEFS

So, we all have beliefs, right? Of course we do. You have beliefs about your family, your company, your boss, and your opportunities in your life. So my question is this: Are the beliefs that you have *true*? Yes or no?

Imagine, just for fun, that there are two men, and these two men—let's call them Perry Noyd and Conn Serned—both call up their wives on the phone and they say, "Hey honey, let's meet out for dinner tonight. Let's meet at our favorite restaurant, you know, the one we got engaged at. Let's meet at 7:00; we'll talk about the day, reconnect, have some dinner, and have some fun. It's going to be great!" So 7:00 p.m. rolls around, and for some reason the ladies aren't there. The husbands aren't worried at first, yet then it's 7:15 . . . 7:30 . . . 7:45 . . . 8:15 . . . 8:45 . . . and still no sign of their wives. The first guy, Perry Noyd, is really upset. He's angry! He's banging on tables; veins are popping out of his neck, he's really mad. He's rehearsing the talking-to his wife's gonna get when she finally decides to show up, and he's practicing his punches for the guy he's sure she's messing around with. The other gentleman, Conn Serned, is very worried—visibly worried—about his wife's safety. He's fidgeting, trying to decide whether his next move is to run home to see that she's all right or just to dial 911. My question is, What's the difference between these two men?

Now, I've heard everything you can imagine. "Aw, Perry is a jerk." "He's insensitive." "He's selfish." "He sounds like my husband." I've heard it all. Yet what it really comes down to is each of those men's beliefs. You see, Perry *believes* his wife is doing something she shouldn't be doing or that she's late because she's thoughtless, and he allows that to make him angry. Conn, on the other hand, believes his wife's a good, loyal, thoughtful person. She's always on time, so if she's not there, something must have happened to her, so he's concerned. I'd say that's fairly obvious.

Now, here's the real question. Which one of these men is right? Well, they both are. If you went into that restaurant and you saw those two men and you said, "Hey guys! Which one of you is right?" How do you think they'd respond? Each one would say, "I am!"

The reason I'm sharing this story with you is that whatever you believe right now about your ability to make a change in your life, make more money, reach your goals, exceed your quota, or make your relationships work is *absolutely true for you* right now.

A WORD FROM A MAN WHO KNEW

Years ago, I had an experience that really opened up my mind to the power of beliefs. I worked for Tony Robbins for six years. I started out with a group of aggressive young sales professionals who went around the country selling tickets to Tony's business seminars. We'd go to a major marketplace such as New York, Chicago, or Los Angeles, and we'd go into companies and make a 30- to 40-minute high-energy, peak-performance presentation based on the customers' needs. Then we'd introduce the event, sell the tickets, and collect money. It was a straight commission job, and I'd never done any public speaking before in my life. Needless to say it was a great growth opportunity for me, and I share more of that story in Chapter 5.

During this time I was so hungry for success that I would meet people I thought were successful and I would ask them to lunch, to dinner, to breakfast. I wanted to figure out what successful people were doing. In one of my meetings in Washington, D.C., there was this 26-year-old guy who was making a quarter-million dollars a year, which was even bigger money then than it is now. He was focused. He was driven. I was impressed. I didn't think he was any smarter than I was, yet he was definitely doing something different to get the results. I asked him if I could buy him some breakfast, and he was a real positive guy and he said, "Sure!" So we met the next morning. We'd only been talking for about ten minutes— about making money, taking it to the next level—when he stopped me and said, "Hey, Dan, can I share something with you?" I said, "Sure!" I was sitting there with my notepad out, ready to learn something from this young guy, and he said, "You know, I don't know what you really want to do with your life, where you really want to be, what your goals are, what you see for yourself, yet I can tell you something right now." I answered, "Yeah. What is it?" I was ready to take some notes, right? He said, "I don't care what you do or how hard you work, you'll never earn $250,000 a year." You can imagine me sitting there going, "Great, thanks." He said, "No, listen, Dan. I really like you. Listen to me very carefully." He said, "You'll never earn $250,000 with that $110,000 belief system you currently have inside your head." In that moment I got it. I really understood what he was saying, because that's the fact. You'll never earn $250,000 with a $100,000 belief system—just as you'll never earn $100,000 with a $50,000 belief system, just as you'll never earn $50,000 with a $10-an-hour belief system. You'll never out earn or outsell your own belief systems.

CHOOSING AND EXCHANGING YOUR BELIEFS

So my question is, What's holding you back right now? What's the disempowering belief that you have, which you must change to take your life or your business to the next level?

I really want you to get this: *Half of the things right now that you believe, whether they're personal or professional, are not true.* And half the things you worry about are never going to happen. So, if you're going to believe something, and it might or might not be true—*believe something positive.*

Suppose you're a salesperson. If you really believed that everybody you talked to was going to buy your product, do you think you'd be in a pretty good mood? I think so. Would you walk with confidence? Would you introduce yourself with a firm handshake? Would you call people back? Well, of course you would.

Well, here's the next question. Even if you really did believe that everybody you met was going to buy your product, would that really happen? Well, probably not. Yet I guarantee you'd make more sales because of the things you were doing. I guarantee that you'd make more sales than the guy who believed that people don't buy from him or that he's not a good salesperson.

So, what's the disempowering belief that you have that's holding you back right now?

In Chapter 2 I'm going to teach you more about how to change those beliefs into an empowering belief. Yet for right now, here's your Action Plan for this chapter:

Identify one of your disempowering beliefs.

This shouldn't be difficult. Most people have a laundry list of negative beliefs that are holding them back. "I don't have the time. I don't have the resources. I don't have a degree. I don't have the experience. I'm not good enough." Do any of these sound familiar? You can achieve anything you're committed to. You can achieve anything you want, yet first you have to start with a foundation for your success—your belief system. So identify that one disempowering belief. If you're in a place where you can write it down, stop and write it down right now. Let's build a strong success foundation. Great job! Go out and take it to The Next Level!

CHAPTER 2

Building Momentum

I'm really excited about this chapter because I'm going to share with you a very simple, yet powerful strategy that's changed the course of my life. This simple strategy has helped me build momentum, take action, and really change my beliefs. I've been teaching this strategy for over a decade, and even when people have heard it before, they thank me because it's a great reminder, because when they use it they really make progress.

It's called the *"As If"* strategy. Simply, acting *"As If."* Acting *as if* you were the person you really want to be.

Let's have some fun for a minute. The fact that you're reading this book means you're open-minded and willing to give it a shot. So play along with me just for a minute. Think about the picture you have for yourself in your mind: the goal you want to achieve, the success you're striving for, and being that person right now that you're striving to be. I mean right now! Suppose you were that person you really want to be—the top sales professional, the amazing parent, the most respected executive, the great leader—whatever you're shooting for. If you were that person right now—in the local papers, the magazines, *USA Today*; the best of the best—how would you be sitting? How would you treat people today? How would you walk? How would you talk? Whom would you call? If you were that person you really want to be, how would you plan your day? How much patience would you have? How confident would you be?

Now a follow-up question: if you knew that in the next ninety days you were really going to achieve what you really wanted to do, whom would you call today? How would you conduct yourself and how much discipline would you have? You know those days when you're absolutely unstoppable? I mean, you know those days, right? Well, if you don't, imagine what it would be like to have one of those days. And then there are those other days when you're just not your best. You're the same person, with the same talent and skills, yet often it's what's going on inside your head that limits your potential.

A MAN WHO WENT BEYOND FIRST IMPRESSIONS

I'm going to tell you a story about a person you know, besides myself, who used the "as if" strategy to catapult his career to the highest level. Now he's not in my business, and probably not in yours, yet everybody knows who he is: Jim Carrey, the comedian. Now, like him or not, I'm sure you'd agree that he's doing pretty well for himself.

Jim Carrey grew up in Canada. His father was an accountant at a major accounting firm; the firm went through some downsizing, and Jim's father lost his job. Times were tough out there, so instead of accounting, Jim's dad had to take a job as a security guard and a janitor. Things didn't get any better, and Jim himself had to go to work as a part-time janitor to help his family make ends meet. Times got still worse, and they lost their home. I remember Jim talking about it at an interview, and he said, "You know, people think that I'm so funny." He said, "I was so funny because I worked so hard to compete with my father. My father's the funniest man on the planet." He said, "I remember when we lost our home. Even [though] the times were so tough, . . . he kept everything so light. He told us to get in the van, that we were going camping, yet we never came home."

So they drove across Canada, and this is how Jim's dad would make the money: He would book Jim to open for bands and close after bands, doing impressions. If you remember when Jim Carrey first came up, he would get on stage and turn his back to the audience, then turn back around, and bam! he'd be Sammy Davis Jr., Clint Eastwood. That's all he used to do, and he was getting known as the next Rich Little.

Well, Carrey built up his reputation around Canada, yet that's not a place to make it big in show biz, so he moved out to Hollywood. As he was doing his thing at the comedy clubs, he said to himself, "Hey! This isn't what I want to do. I don't want to do impressions and be the next Rich Little. I want to be a comedian. I want to do *my* stuff." So he went out on stage one night in Los Angeles, and instead of doing the impressions, he pulled out his stuff—his wacky humor. It didn't go over so well. If you were in the audience, having bought a ticket with the expectation of seeing a great impressionist, and you got "Fireman Bill," you might not be thrilled either. Carrey was literally booed off the stage, and the owners of the club told him to go back to doing impressions: "That's what the people want to see." Carrey went home and was feeling very low. He felt like quitting the business. He went to Mulholland Drive, which looks over Los Angeles, and he stood there overlooking the city just imagining he was the king of comedy. He went home, still feeling kind of down, turned on the TV late at night, and he saw a guy talking about acting *as if you already are who you want to be.*

I'm going to repeat that for you. He saw a guy talking about acting as if you already are who you want to be, and, bam! it just hit him. He took out his checkbook and wrote a check to Jim Carrey, from Jim Carrey, in the amount of $10 million; postdated the check for six months; and on the memo line in the lower left-hand corner, wrote "For acting services rendered." And he went out and he showed this check to everybody that he met, friends, actors, agents, people walking down the street, "Hey! Have you seen my check? Ten million dollars!"

Now that sounds funny because it's Jim Carrey. Yet imagine you doing that right now, telling your friends, "Hey! I was just reading Dan Lier's book, *The 10 Minute Coach*, and I just got a check for $10 million. What do you think? Yeah, I know it's from me; what do you think?" Your friends would probably think you're nuts.

Yet here's what Jim Carrey said to himself: "If I absolutely knew beyond a shadow of a doubt, I mean, with 100 percent certainty"—now remember that a belief is a sense of certainty—"that in six months, bam, this check was going to be good; $10 million was going right in my checking account . . . if I knew that was going to happen, how many hours would I spend making ridiculous faces in front of this mirror? How many people would I tell I'm the funniest man in the world? How many auditions would I go after? And of course, how many nos would I be willing to hear if I absolutely knew this check was going to be good?"

And of course, the rest is history. Jim Carrey became the highest-paid comedian in the world. When Jim Carrey used the "as if" strategy, he walked in to auditions in a different way. He was acting as if he was the best, so he walked in differently, he talked differently, and he did things differently.

YOU, AS IF YOU ARE WHO YOU WANT TO BE

I don't know where you are personally right now—what you want to achieve, what goals and dreams you have for yourself— yet I can tell you this: If you finish this chapter and act *as if* you already are the person you want to be, *your life will never be the same.* Because if you were, right now, that person you really envision yourself being, what would you do today? How would you treat people? What kind of attitude would you have? Whom would you call?

I've used this strategy in business to catapult my career. Yet I've had the most impact in my personal life. One of my personal goals was to be an outstanding father; the kind of father who creates an environment where my kids can talk to me about things—school, their challenges, sex, drugs, all the things that come into kids' lives. And I remember living in Los Angeles, coming home from work when my son was four and my daughter was two. I walked in the door, and, of course, the kids were excited to see me. Daniel was jumping around, shouting, "Daddy's home," and Zoë was dancing, and, of course, they wanted to play. I remember saying, "Hey kids, just give me thirty minutes. I need to check my e-mails, make a couple calls; just thirty minutes." Well, thirty minutes turned into sixty, and, of course, two hours later I was tucking my kids into bed. Is that what an outstanding father does? No way.

So I remember catching myself and reminding myself of what kind of father that I really wanted to be, and I made a decision to act *as if.* I put a sticky note in my car that said, "Act as if," to remind me to act *as if* I were the best father in the world. So I came home the next day and it was pretty predictable, like *Groundhog Day.* Daniel was jumping up around, shouting, "Daddy's home," Zoë was dancing, and of course, they wanted to play. My mind started replaying my old patterns. I was thinking to myself, "Oh, just give me thirty minutes." Yet this time I was prepared and I said to myself, "Well, maybe I'm not the best father in the world right now, yet if I were an outstanding father, what would I do right now?" Then of course the answer was obvious: I'd play with my kids. So I put down my briefcase, took off my tie, and started playing with my kids, rolling around, having fun, building their self-esteem, and showing them love. And what happened was that I started building my own references about me being an outstanding father.

Now Daniel's ten and Zoë's eight and I am an outstanding father. Remember from Chapter 1 that beliefs drive our behavior. So at this point, of course, I spend time with my son, ask him questions about his life and his interests, or just play catch, because that's what an outstanding father does. Of course I tell my daughter she's amazing, beautiful, and intelligent and that she can do anything, because that's what a great father does. Use the "as if" strategy, and it'll change the direction of your life.

So, here's your Action Plan for this chapter. Let's start changing a disempowering belief and build some momentum right now.

Get an index card or a sticky note, write the words "Act as if"
on it, and put it up.

Put the note up in your car or in your bathroom—or, better
yet, make multiple note cards and put them up in several
places. The reason this is necessary is that the "as if" strategy
is not yet conditioned as a part of your psychology. You've got
to keep it in front of your face to remind yourself until it
becomes a habit.

When you finish reading this chapter (just a few lines
away!), act *as if* you are that person you really want to be. Show
up strong, confident, and full of certainty. Great job! This is
the day you make the decision to act as if you are the person
you want to be. Think about yourself and where you want to
be in the next five, ten years. Act as if you are that person
today. Walk that way, talk that way. Great job! Go out and take
it to The Next Level!

CHAPTER 3

The Power of a Winning Attitude

So, how are you feeling today? Are you excited about your day? Let's talk about your attitude. I love talking about having a winning attitude, because it's one of the few things in life that you and I can control. We don't have control over the weather, the stock market, interest rates, taxes, or traffic. Yet we do have control over our attitude. You have the ability to wake up in the morning, put your feet on the floor, and make a decision about how you're going to show up that day.

Attitude is one of the little things in life that makes the big difference. Trust me on this one. In my line of work I meet so many people with all the talent and skills, all the fancy degrees; yet they have a poor attitude and they're struggling. On the other hand, I've met people who don't have a college degree, who've been dealt some challenging cards, so to speak, yet they have an incredible attitude and they're really making things happen.

Napoleon Hill, in his timeless book *Think and Grow Rich*, talks about the power of a pleasing personality. Here's what's interesting. Our personal and business lives have changed so much with technology and e-commerce, yet something as simple as a *winning attitude* can make or break your vision.

It's funny to me how some businesspeople just don't understand this concept. I remember when I was kicking off the national sales meeting for a *Fortune* 100 company. I was to speak at 9:00 for about an hour so as to get them really fired up for the president and CEO to lay out their new vision. I remember walking out to a couple of people before the event; they were sitting in their chairs waiting for the event to get started, and I walked up and greeted one guy with, "Hey, good morning! How're you doing?" His response was, "Ah, can't complain. I mean, no one listens anyway." I said, "Great! Keep up the good work," walked over to another guy, and said, "Hey, how're you doing?" *His* response was, "Ah, same old s[tuff], different day." I said, "Fantastic!" These people wonder why they're not making it happen! They wonder why people aren't attracted to them.

Here is some bonus information for you, and you can take this to the bank. *People like to be around people who make them feel good.* I'm going to repeat that for you. People like to be around people who make them feel good.

LEVEL 4 OR LEVEL 11?

You get out of life what you put into it. If you want to be respected, then be respectful. If you want to be loved, then be more loving. If you want to be around people who are positive, then you need to be positive around other people. It's that simple.

Let me ask you a question. On a scale of zero to ten, ten being the most important and zero not being important at all, how important is having a great attitude? My experience says most people respond by saying ten or even 11. Here's what I need to remind people on occasion: We live in the greatest country in the world; a country with opportunities and freedoms that, quite frankly, are priceless, and yet some people show up every single day at their opportunity and operate at a Level 4 and 5, and guess what kind of results they get? That's right, four or five. It's not brain surgery. You get out of life what you put into it.

In the previous paragraph I said *opportunity* instead of *job* because, in all my travels and speaking events, no one has ever told me they were forced to take the job they currently have. It was their choice. They made the decision to accept that specific job; thus, in my mind, it's an opportunity. So why wouldn't you show up at your opportunity being your best?

Let me use a sports analogy. Years ago, Michael Jordan was the best basketball player in the world. My background is basketball as well. If I were to play Michael Jordan in a game of basketball when we were both at our prime, at what level would I need to be on that scale of zero to ten to have a chance to compete against Michael Jordan? You may be thinking to yourself, "15" or "20." Thanks for your confidence!! Yet I think we'd all agree that I'd have to be at my very best to have a chance to compete at that level. We all agree with that.

Yet many people go to work—or rather, their opportunity— each and every day and operate at a Level 4 or a Level 5 out of 10. And that's exactly what they get: four or five results out of ten. *To maximize whatever opportunity you're pursuing you must make a decision to show up with a great attitude.*

Some News about Your Issues

I want to give you some news that I believe will really help you put things into perspective. Would you agree that, if I were to interview each and every person you knew, I'd find that each one would, most likely, have a few issues or challenges going on? What do you think? Well, probably so. Some have more issues than others, yet everyone has them—some big, some small, some serious, some imaginary, some not so serious—yet we all have issues.

Now here is the news about your issues, and this is meant with the best intentions. This is the secret: *Nobody cares.* And I mean that sincerely, yet with all due respect: *nobody cares about your issues.* They may like you, they may care about you, yet— except for a few really close friends and loved ones who know you really well—the people you deal with *don't want to hear about your stuff!*

I'll give you an example. Let's say your company has hired me to do a kickoff meeting or some kind of presentation, and your company president is introducing me. He's saying, "Dan Lier is one of the top speakers in the country; he's done over

3,000 presentations worldwide, he works with the best of the best—Brian Tracy, Dennis Waitley, Og Mandino, Tony Robbins—and he's here today to share some strategies to blast us off. Let's hear it for Mr. Dan Lier!" Everybody's clapping, and I come out and, in a very low-energy, slow monotone I say:

> Ah, hey how's everybody doing today . . . oh wow, I'm tired . . . um, my name's Dan Lier and I'm a peak performance coach . . . and I'm the author of *The 10 Minute Coach* . . . and I'm really . . . excited to be here today . . . um . . . we're going to get started today and really talk about success . . . and I'm usually a little bit better than this . . . but my wife and I are having a few issues . . . and . . . ah, you know . . . it's bringing me down, and . . . uh, my son's having a few challenges in school and . . . um, my daughter's dating an Eminem wannabe . . .

Now that skit's officially over! Can you imagine if I came out like that? I mean, if you were seated in the audience, what would you be saying to yourself? Probably something like, "Hey get this guy out of here. *He's* a peak performance coach? Whatever you paid him, get your money back." The fact of the matter is, from a humanistic standpoint you might say, "Hey, I think Dan's a nice guy. I like him." Yet quite frankly, you don't care about my issues. I mean, does that make sense? You have your own issues. Why do you want to hear about mine?

In addition, the dangerous part about sharing your stuff with others, or just having a sour attitude, is that people make an association about you based on your attitude. Remember back in high school when we learned about Pavlov and his dogs? He had dogs in a controlled environment. He put out some dog food and rang a bell. They smelled the food and started to salivate. He repeated the process: put out the food, ring the bell, and they'd salivate. Then pretty soon he just rang the bell without putting out the food, yet the dogs started to salivate anyway, because they had created an association between food and the bell. They were *conditioned*. The same thing takes place each and every day at work and at home in regards to you and your attitude.

Let's say I was hired to come in and give a presentation, or perform a weekly sales meeting at your company, and every time I came in I was in a great mood, teaching people solid strategies, smiling, excited about life, giving people sincere compliments. After a short period of time you'd get an association about me. You'd be saying, "Man, I like that guy. He's positive." Pretty soon what would happen is that all you'd have to do is see my face, hear my voice, or even see my business card, and you'd start to feel good. You'd get conditioned to my attitude. The reason I say so is that—I guarantee you right now—there's somebody in your business or your personal life where all you have to do is see their face, hear their voice, and you start to feel tired and depressed. You probably have a picture of that person in your head right now. Have you ever been out to lunch with someone and afterwards felt like taking a nap? No one likes to hear complaining or negativity.

The Power of Associations

I think about this quite a bit because associations and attitudes are so powerful. When I come home from work, I hit the garage door opener and my wife, Tammy, hears the garage door open, depending on where she is in the house. When she hears the garage door start to open, what goes through her mind? Does she hear the garage door and say, "Yay! All right! Dan's home!" That's what I'm working on. That's what I want her to say. Or does she hear the garage door and say, "Aw, geez, Dan's home"? It's not something she has to think about. She doesn't hear the garage door and say to herself, "Hmm, I wonder how I feel about Dan today?" No, it's conditioned in her body. It's an automated response based on how I've been treating her over the days, weeks, or months. It's the same thing with you. People are making associations about you every single day. At work, or at home, are you giving people a positive association with you or a negative one?

Remember, people like to be around people who make them feel good. So if you haven't been the positive role model that you'd like to be, make a decision to turn it around today. I mean, hey, if not now, then when? I know it's easier said than done, so here's the key: People who tend not to be in such a great mood typically have their attention focused on what they don't have or what's not going right in their lives. If you're consistently focused on what's wrong with everything, you're not going to be so pleasant to be around. It's like the old saying, "Is the glass half full or half empty?" The challenge with you looking at the glass half empty is that it doesn't do anything positive for you. It doesn't help you get closer to your goals.

So, here's your Action Plan for this chapter:

Take just a minute and think about all the great things in your life, all your relationships, all the people who love you and care about you. Think about all the opportunities you have, all the freedom you have to make choices, all the things you've accomplished in your life, and think about it.

The glass is more than half full. It always is. So you just have to remember that. *So let's make a decision today to be your best.* Be someone whom others want to be around.

So, today, operate at a Level 10. I mean, come on! You can do it just for one day. If you do it too many days in a row, you'll get way too successful and have more friends than you know what to do with, so let's just take it one day at a time. Can you do that? Can you do it just one day at a Level 10? Of course you can. So, congratulations on taking your first step. Go out and take it to The Next Level!

CHAPTER 4

Overcoming Adversity

Let me begin this session by asking you a question. Do you think that, between now and a couple of months from now, you might be presented with a few challenges in your life? Well, the answer is obviously yes. We all have challenges. We all have issues, and we're all faced with adversity. Knowing that adversity is inevitable, the real question is, How effective are you at overcoming adversity? Overcoming adversity and building yourself back up is what I call a success pattern. You see, that's really the key.

My parents were divorced when I was six. From age six to twelve I lived with my mother and sister, and we really struggled financially. We spent time on government assistance programs; and I wore my aunt's clothes to school, which was not what you'd call positive for my self-esteem. As a result, my focus was to work really hard, go to school, get a degree, and make a lot of money, because I had that belief that if you made a lot of money you wouldn't have any problems.

Needless to say, that belief of mine wasn't true. As a matter of fact, the more money people have, the more challenges typically come their way. And what I've learned from top performers is that they simply overcome that adversity more quickly. You see, we have a couple of choices. When something goes wrong in our lives—someone lies to you, someone cheats you, someone disappoints you, or you just have a major crisis— you can either make that challenge bigger and make it last a long time, or look at it for what it is, address it, handle it, and make yourself stronger. I know: Easier said than done.

Well, first of all, let's understand there's a place for adversity. That is, adversity is a part of life, and the product of you overcoming that adversity will make you stronger and arm you with the ability to make things happen. That's one of the challenges today I see as a parent. I see many kids who don't know how to overcome adversity. Someone's always there to bail them out. The problem with that is that overcoming adversity builds character and self-esteem, and these young kids will never have that feeling that, no matter what comes their way, they can always make it happen on their own. Self-esteem is not something you can buy in a store.

OPPORTUNITIES FROM ADVERSITIES

James Cash Penney was, as you might guess, the founder of the JCPenney department stores. When a journalist asked Penney about his success, he replied, "I would not have amounted to anything if I hadn't been forced to handle adversity." Now, here's a belief that I'd like you to adopt: *Opportunity comes from adversity.* Here are some more examples.

❐ Before the Civil War a gentleman named Edmund McIlhenny operated a sugar plantation in Louisiana. Yankee troops invaded the area, and McIlhenny was forced to run. When he came back two years later, his sugar fields were ruined. One of the few things left were some hot Mexican peppers that had reseeded themselves near the garden. At this point in his life, McIlhenny was living day to day. He was struggling. He was really challenged. He started experimenting with the ground peppers to make some sauce that would liven up his bland diet. Well, the sauce he came up with over 100 years ago is known all over the world today as Tabasco sauce, and the McIlhenny Company and the Tabasco business are still run by his family.

❐ Henry Ford went broke five times before becoming successful.

☐ Beethoven rose above his deafness to become one of the world's best composers.

☐ As an elementary student, James Earl Jones stuttered so badly that he used notes to communicate. Now, of course, he's known for his powerful and impactful voice.

Read and reread this carefully: *Greatness springs from adversity.* The problems you are experiencing right now are setting the foundation for your success.

ADVERSITY: TROUBLE OR CHALLENGE

So, let's talk about how to overcome adversity and get you back on track to being your best.

First of all, I've found that most people have negative patterns associated with handling adversity: trouble, problems, issues, or distress. Let's start now by giving such problems, issues, and adversities a new label: *challenges.* You might respond, "Well that's silly. Why would I want to do that?" Our language is so powerful, and how we label things can affect how we think. And, of course, how we think affects what we do. "Problems," "issues," "adversity," and so on carry a label of struggle, something big or overwhelming. When we think about a "challenge," on the other hand, it really doesn't send us into a tailspin. Most people like a good challenge. If you're a golfer, you look forward to a challenging hole. So what makes your life any different?

PERFORMANCE QUESTIONS

Here's what's really interesting. We all talk to ourselves—some of us more than others, yet, we all do it. As the joke has it, "It's when you answer yourself, that's when you need to worry"—or, rather, *how* you answer yourself. Generally speaking, most of our internal dialogue is not positive. When most people are faced with a challenge, their internal dialogue is on auto response. When they ask themselves questions, they ask negative questions—questions that don't promote action or growth, such as "Why does this always happen to me?" or "Why don't

I ever get a break?" They get into what I call the "Why can't I's."—"Why can't I do this," "Why can't I have that." Then they answer themselves, and it goes on and on and on. When you ask these types of questions, your brain responds with a negative answer. That's how your brain works. Ask a negative question, get a negative response.

Remember, 90 percent of your success—in business, life, and relationships—is your psychology. Let me give you an example. Have you ever had the desire to start going to the gym and get in better shape? Well, let me ask you another question. Do you know how to get to the gym? Well, of course you do. Yet getting yourself there; that's the challenge! You know how, yet getting yourself to do it is something different. Again, it's your psychology. You know that challenges are going to come your way. It's how you handle them that determine your success and progress as a person.

Here's what the top performers do to overcome adversity and build a success pattern: they ask themselves what I call *performance questions* instead of negative ones. Performance questions are questions that cause your brain to be proactive and to find the solution to your situation. For example: "How can I use this to make me stronger?" "How can I overcome the situation like a champion?" "What can I learn from this to make me more powerful?" "How can I use this to make me a better person, a better parent, a better husband, or a better wife?" A performance question is typically a "how can I" or "what can I" question instead of a "why can't I" question.

Remember, you were designed for success, yet often times people just mentally download the wrong information. Suppose you set a goal of going to the gym four times this week, yet you only go twice. If you go into the normal negative pattern, you start with, "Aw, geez, why can't I ever get myself to go to the gym?" or "Why am I such a loser?" or "Why can't I ever lose weight?" or "Why don't I ever follow through?" Your brain responds with negative answers, which makes you feel worse. You get tired of all this, *so you order some pizza and you eat a bag of cookies* to drown out your sorrows, leaving you in the same disempowering pattern.

Yet suppose you use performance questions instead. You didn't make it to the gym, yet instead of beating yourself up you ask, "What can I learn from this so that next week I'll get to the gym all four times?" or "How can I rearrange my activities to make it easier for myself to go to the gym?" These are questions that cause your brain to respond with some action steps towards your goal. Here's how I might answer those questions:

❑ *What can I learn from this so that next week I'll get to the gym all four times?* I don't break business appointments with my clients, do I? So let's see. I'm going to schedule my workouts in the same book I use for business appointments.

❑ *How can I rearrange my activities to make it easier for myself to go to the gym?* Let's see, Wednesdays are typically a bit light. I'll schedule a workout on Wednesday at noon. I'll also schedule a workout one day of the week in the morning before work.

By asking yourself performance questions, you came up with solutions to support your growth and progress as a human being. That's what a top performer does. Ask a winning question; get a game plan for success.

So here's your Action Plan for this chapter:

If you're going through some challenges right now, come up with a couple of performance questions to get yourself back on track and moving in the right direction. "What can I learn from this?" "How can this make me stronger?" "How can I use this to make me a better leader?"

We've already determined that adversity or challenges are part of your life. You can make them last indefinitely—at the expense of your state of mind, your job, and your relationships—or you can shorten your downtime by asking performance questions that cause you take action in the right direction, which, in turn, builds your success patterns.

As I've said, 90 percent of your success is your psychology. The better you are at handling or managing your psychology, the more successful you're going to be. So you can do it.

Whatever challenges you're going through right now, ask some performance questions. Work yourself through the process. I know it's not easy. It's never easy to rise above what knocks most people down. You can do it! Write down a couple of performance questions and start moving in the right direction. *Remember, tough times don't last, tough people do.* So go out and take it to The Next Level!

CHAPTER 5

Goal Setting and Vision

So, where do you want to go?

Where do you want to be in the next year, five years, or even ten years? Do you have a picture in your mind of where you want to be?

I'm sure you are familiar with goal setting, yet I'm wondering whether you are really doing it? When was the last time you set goals and really created a vision for yourself for the next five or ten years?

If you've missed the opportunity, no worries . . . let's get started today. I'm going to share with you The Next Level in goal setting and really creating a vision for yourself.

When I talk to people who've achieved greatness in their lives, they've all seen the picture of success before it's happened. They've seen it in their mind. In previous chapters I talked about the power of beliefs. Now I'm going to talk about creating a vision along with your daily goals.

The first time Andre Agassi won Wimbledon, he was interviewed right after the match, and he was asked, "So, how does it feel to win your first Wimbledon?" He responded by saying, "Just like I imagined hundreds of times in my mind." Wherever it is you want to go, you must create and keep a vivid mental picture in your head of you achieving your goal. The brain is an amazing, complex tool that moves in the direction of your most dominant thoughts and pictures.

YOUR COACH'S VISION

Remember the story I began to tell in Chapter 1 about how I worked for Tony Robbins, going from city to city promoting his seminars, living entirely on commissions from ticket sales. We went to five cities a year, and I did that for for six years. So, over a six-year period I lived in thirty cities. That's a long time for that position. Most people came on the road with us and lasted for about 18 months. In addition, during the first year I was out on the road, I met an amazing woman named Tammy. She was hired and worked along with me. We started dating, got married, and had two children during that six-year period. Most people cannot imagine picking up and moving every couple of months for six years; finding a new doctor, a dentist, a hair stylist, finding your way around—and, from Tammy's perspective, having two or three different obstetricians throughout one pregnancy. People always ask, "How did you do it?"

The only way I stayed focused and didn't find a reason to quit and do something else is by having a clear picture in my mind of why I was there and what I needed to learn to get me where I wanted to go. Believe me, there were plenty of times when things were tough and our commitment and resilience were tested. Yet having a clear picture in my mind of where I wanted to be allowed me to stay focused and perform. Things continued to progress. In the middle of my third year I had established myself as one of the top performers and was appointed to be the team leader and manager. Now I was responsible for hiring and training all the speakers who would go on the road and sell with us. I traveled with the team and I continued to sell, hire, and train, and our team was setting records in ticket sales. Soon after that, our son Daniel was born. We were still on the road with our sales team, and during this time many talented people had come and gone. Yet I knew that I had more skills to acquire before I was ready to go, so I kept the vision clearly in my mind. As a result of my focus, opportunities came, and my skills went through the roof.

In addition to his one-day business seminar, Tony had other events called Wealth Mastery and Financial Power, which were three- and four-day events that, of course, had a much higher price point attached to them. To sell these events, they put together guest events in major cities. Essentially, the marketing department would advertise a financial power guest event, and people would come for a three-hour preview of an upcoming financial power program. The events had anywhere from 500 to 1,000 attendees, depending on the city. The funny part about it was that some of those people were under the impression that Tony himself was going to be there. So when they introduced the speaker with "Let's hear it for Mr. Dan Lier!" many of the people in the audience were saying, "Who in the heck's this guy?" So I had to introduce myself, capture the audience, entertain them, educate them, and then enroll them in a three- or four-day event. When people are expecting Tony Robbins and they get Dan Lier, it has to get really good, really fast. I did at least one or two guest events just like that per month for over a year and a half. My skills really expanded, and those were the skills I needed to take my career to the next level.

When my daughter Zoë was born, I knew it was about time for me to take the next step. Tony asked me to come over to the corporate office and run his seminar division and sit in on his executive team, which was a great opportunity, yet it really wasn't the vision I had in my mind. Tony and I met up at the Four Seasons Hotel in New York City, and I told him it was time for me to do my own thing. We thanked each other for the friendship and opportunity, and then I launched Level 10 International, a speaking, training, and coaching company. With over 3,000 live presentations under my belt, and experience as a manager and a coach, I was ready to go.

What was the picture in my mind? It was to be one of the world's most sought-after speakers and coaches, and I knew I had to pay the price to get there. Now, I perform numerous speaking events every month and I've built a team of success coaches who are second to none. The only way that I was able to keep on traveling and moving my family for six years was the *image of success that I kept in my mind.*

Your Vision

So my question is, what's the picture you have for yourself in your mind? If you haven't done so already, create a vivid mental picture in your mind of you doing what you really want to do. Maybe it's sportscasting, maybe selling real estate, maybe owning and operating a restaurant. Whatever your dream is, create the picture and keep it in your mind. Make it vivid. What are you wearing? What are you doing? *Make it real.* That's the first step.

The second step is simple, yet this strategy will get you where you want to go. I spoke briefly about goal setting at the beginning of this chapter, and I asked you whether you have one- to five- to ten-year goals. The reality is that most people don't. Setting goals is quite predictable. When do most people set their goals? That's right: New Year's Eve. "This is the year, baby! I'm going to make it happen! I'm going to quit smoking. I'm going to lose 25 pounds; increase my income by 40 percent. I'm going to spend some time with my family. I'm going to make it happen!" I've heard it all.

Now my follow-up question is this: When do most people check those same goals again? That's right: *next* New Year's Eve. Most people don't hit their long-term goals because they lose their focus and stop taking actions that are necessary for them to win.

So here's the key: When implementing a change or creating momentum, you must set *daily* goals. When you hit your daily goals, the rest of it's going to take care of itself. If you want to lose 30 pounds, the thought of that could be overwhelming. Yet if you check with a doctor and implement a daily goal of, maybe, keeping the day's calories down to 1,500 to 2,000, you'll find yourself making strides even if you don't get in as much exercise as you should. If you're in sales and you have certain sales goals or account goals, you'll always hit your mark if you break down your activities into daily goals. For example, if you always made ten calls a day; ten cold calls— I mean, no matter what, no matter how bad your day was— let's face it: That's 50 calls a week. That's 200 cold calls a month. Now it doesn't sound like a lot, yet I guarantee most people aren't doing that. A lot of things can come up, yet if you hit your daily goals you're always going to have enough prospects.

Success is not an accident, and most of the time success doesn't allow for any shortcuts. So, here's your Action Plan, which is in two steps for this chapter:

Step 1: *Create that vivid picture in your mind of you being who you really want to be, and keep it there.*

Step 2: *Create daily goals for your success, and mark them on your calendar or day organizer. Put a special calendar in your office or on your refrigerator door and mark the days when you hit your daily goals.*

The image of you being successful, the image in your mind, will keep you focused, and the daily goals will allow you to make constant progress towards your goal. Great job! Go out and take it to The Next Level!

CHAPTER 6

Overcoming Failure

Have you experienced some failure recently? Or does the thought of failing paralyze you from taking action on your ideas? When I ask people about failure and what they associate with failure, I hear things like, "disappointment, discouragement, setback, letdown, I'm a loser!"

How about you? If I were to ask you what it means to fail, how would you respond? Well, if your response was similar to the ones you just heard, there's a good chance you are not maximizing your potential as a human being, and that affects your self-esteem, your self-image, and your results. Here's an alternative perspective on failure.

SUCCEEDING THROUGH FAILING

Years ago, I met a very successful businessman in Atlanta. I was honored and privileged to sit down with him, and I was anxious to learn some ideas from someone who had created multi-millions in his life. So I asked him, "What advice could you give me that you feel that many people just don't understand?" Of course, I had my note pad out; ready to take some notes. He responded in a very upbeat manner: "Oh, that's easy," he said. *"Fail as much as you can as fast as you can."* I smiled, and my body language must have indicated that I really didn't understand, because he asked, "Did you get that?" and said it again: "Fail as much as you can as fast as you can." He said, *"The only reason I'm sitting here getting interviewed by you is that I've failed more than anyone else I know. The difference is what failure means to me and how I respond to it.*"

What I learned that day, and what I continue to recognize in other high achievers, is their understanding of failure. You see, failure doesn't mean that you're a loser, or you're an under-achiever. *Failure* is simply a word attached to the results you achieved when those results weren't the results you were shooting for. When you understand that there's a value in failing and it's a necessary step toward succeeding, then it's easier to wrap your head around it.

You were designed to succeed, period. The only way that you have a chance to succeed is by doing new things, taking new steps in a new direction, or doing something that you're not already doing. When you don't get the result you're looking for, you've learned something: you've learned what doesn't work. And as long as you're committed to your out-come, now you've a better understanding of how to get there.

Most people have heard the story of one of the greatest inventors in history. Yet he was also one of the greatest failures. Thomas Edison, in his quest to create the incandescent light bulb, failed between 5,000 and 10,000 times, depending on which piece of literature you read. Can you imagine that? Failing 10,000 times? I mean, come on! Most people try some-thing a couple times and they quit. They just concede and they say, "Oh, I guess it just isn't for me." A young journalist, inter-viewing Edison, inquired, "Mr. Edison, why do you continue to waste grant money when you know the human race was designed to go through life with a kerosene lamp?" and Edison replied, he said, "Son, you just don't understand success." He said, "I haven't failed 10,000 times. I found 10,000 ways not to make a light bulb." When you use failure as a learning tool and take your experience and apply it to your vision, you're one step closer. Read this carefully. *If you've just experienced some failure in your life, congratulations!* You're one step closer to where you want to go.

THE ONLY WAY TO FAIL

The only way you can *really* fail is not to put yourself on the line, not to go outside your comfort zone. A person who never fails is really the failure.

I believe that many people have been programmed to fail by being taught that failure is unacceptable.

Think about our school system—which, by the way, was designed during the industrial age, when people were being educated and programmed to work at a factory. We have a grading system based on a few measurable scales, the bell curve, or percentages that tell you whether you are successful. Think about your grade school or high school experience. If you got As, you got treated with respect by parents and teachers and sometimes even by classmates. What if you made below-average grades? How were you treated then? Probably grounded at home and looked down upon at school because you had a specific letter attached to your work. You were considered a failure, and people came to associate you with failure.

With the belief that failing makes you a failure as a person, who wants to put himself or herself in a position to fail? The challenge is that the method of grading was developed back in the industrial age, and we are no longer in the industrial age. We're in the *entrepreneurial age*, where *wealth and success come to those who put themselves at risk.* So many young people graduate from school and go out into the real world afraid to do something, pursue something, or take steps in a certain direction because they don't want to fail. They find themselves stuck or paralyzed in their own interpretation of what failure means.

THE MEANING OF FAILURE

Understand this very clearly: No one likes to fail. *Yet, what failure means to you will either fuel you or hold you back.* What if you knew that failing was a necessary step to you reaching your goals? Would you be willing to play under those conditions? I think so.

Not long ago, I met with Magic Johnson in his Beverly Hills office. We were talking about some business. I had the good fortune to play numerous pick up games (basketball) with and against Magic when I was in college, of course, everybody knows Magic from his basketball wizardry. Yet, he's one of the most respected entrepreneurs in the country. Do you think he's had some setbacks? You bet he has. And I firmly believe that his mindset, his athletic background, and his understanding of the meaning of failure have really allowed him to succeed in the business world, just as he succeeded on the basketball court. He's failed numerous times, yet he understands what it takes to win.

Remember, as I've said before, 90 percent of your success is your psychology: how you handle the situations. So here's your Action Plan for this chapter:

Think about a specific failure you've had and answer the following questions:

1. *What did you learn during that experience that you can apply to future opportunities?*
2. *How has that experience made you wiser, or stronger?*
3. *Can you use that experience to motivate you, to take action once again?*

That's the key to overcoming failure. Remember that failing isn't personal, it's not you; it's simply a result. So use failure as a learning tool.

Here's my question as we close this chapter: Whatever picture you have in your head about where you want to be—if you knew that you had to fail over ten times to achieve you goal, would you still do it? Would you still go after it?

If the answer is yes, then here's my follow-up question. Keeping in mind that you will have to fail at least ten times before you reach your goal, will you want that to take three years, five years, ten years, or twenty years? I think most people would say, "Whoa! If failing's part of my success, let's get it over with quick so I can get on with it"—echoing my conversation with the gentleman in Atlanta: Fail as much as you can as fast as you can.

I hope this session has helped you understand the psychology necessary for you to reach your goals. Remember, you are designed for success. Keep your eyes on your target and learn along the way. Have an amazing journey, and take it to The Next Level!

PART 2
Selling at the Next Level

CHAPTER 7

The Psychology of Selling

I've spent my entire life in the game of selling. I have total respect for sales professionals and what they do, because, quite frankly, nothing happens in this world until something gets sold. Sales is one of the most rewarding professions in the world, and it can be one of the cruelest, most humbling professions as well.

Even if you don't have the word "sales" in your job description, you'll find this part valuable. Selling—influencing others—is part of all walks of life in some form or another. Whether as a top-tier sales professional, as a parent, as a worker, or as a citizen, you'll find these chapters apply in more areas of your life than you may think.

There are many different selling philosophies, addressed to the different components of the sale from cold calling to closing, and you can be successful using more than one of these approaches. Yet the key to selling is really on the mental side of things. It's your psychology. When you break down sales into its components, it's pretty simple: cold calling, cultivation, finding needs, building value, presenting your product, closing, and, of course, getting the reorder. All of these are learned skills. What separates the top professionals from those who struggle, however, is their psychology. This section addresses the psychology necessary to take action and create success in the game of selling and the game of life.

My background's in selling, yet I spent six years working with Tony Robbins giving thousands of presentations and training sessions and coaching premier sales professionals. When I launched Level 10 International (a speaking, training, and coaching company), I continued to attract high-profile coaching clients, many of whom were in the profession of selling. This section is a compilation of success strategies I've learned from the best of the best in selling. Each chapter is designed to give a quick, six- to ten-minute coaching session on various success selling strategies. You can get a quick coaching session before you walk into the office, before you make that cold call, or just on your way to work. I used this approach in my CD product, *The 10 Minute Coach*, and the feedback has been incredible. I mean, people are busy—on the phone making calls—and a quick, ten-minute session fits perfectly into the busy life of sales professionals. Welcome to The Next Level, and let's get started!

CHAPTER 8

Attitude and Enthusiasm

Over the past ten years I've presented to and trained hundreds of thousands of sales professionals, and along the way I've seen many great ones. They were the leaders in their companies. Quite frankly, they didn't all have superior selling skills, yet they all had an outstanding attitude, and they lived their lives with enthusiasm. And I'll let you know up front that I've never, ever, met a sales superstar who was negative or a naysayer, or who went through life thinking the glass was half empty.

My college basketball team won two straight national titles. We had a great basketball coach, Bill Morse, who was recently inducted into the Kansas Sports Hall of Fame. In our locker room he had posted a quote from Ralph Waldo Emerson: "Nothing great was ever achieved without enthusiasm." As I was walking out onto the court before practice, he'd say, "Hey Lier! How you feelin' today?" I was 20 years old at the time, and I'd say, "Oh, I'm all right." He'd say, "Well, if you don't feel great—*fake it*. It's time for practice, and practice makes champions."

If you don't feel great, fake it. I use that to this day. I learned a lot from Coach Morse, because he was always challenging my mental toughness and my ability to respond under adverse circumstances. And, quite frankly, that's what being a winner is all about: being positive when things are tough, being positive when things aren't going your way.

It's easy to be in a great mood when things are going well. When you just had a great month or you closed a great deal, it's easy to be happy. What about when times are tough—when you just lost a sale, when someone deceives you, when someone lies or doesn't follow through? What do you do then? How do you treat people then?

ATTITUDE IS PART OF THE JOB

As a sales professional, I believe that having a great attitude is part of your job. You chose the game of sales, and of course you want to win. To be the best and maximize your abilities, you must be the type of person who doesn't allow outside influences to interrupt your attitude. If you don't want to raise your standards and approach each day with enthusiasm, my suggestion is to change your profession—maybe to something that doesn't require any interaction with people. Seriously, an analogy would be a basketball player who doesn't want to get in shape. He doesn't feel like running up and down the floor. It just doesn't fit. How much success do you think that player will have? Obviously, not much. It's the same for you in regards to your attitude and playing the game of sales. To be successful, influence your prospects, build rapport, and close deals, you must be someone people like to be around.

Here is some bonus information for you today that you can take to the bank. People like to be around people who make them feel good. I'm going repeat that. *People like to be around people that make them feel good.* Doesn't that make sense? Why would you want to hang around someone who brings you down?

WHICH ONE WOULD YOU BUY FROM?

So here's my question. As a consumer, all things being equal, product and price, whom would you buy from: the sales professional with the great attitude, or the one who can tend to get a little cynical or sarcastic, even sour? Well, the choice is obvious.

Now, here's the next question. Again, you're the consumer. There are two products, both similar in features and benefits, and one's a bit more expensive. Yet the more expensive product is being presented to you by a sales professional who has an amazing attitude, and he makes your buying experience enjoyable. The other person has a slightly more inexpensive product, yet you get the feeling that person presenting it is doing it just for a job. Whom do you buy from?

According to the research, 88 percent of Americans will pay more for their purchases if their sales professionals have enthusiasm for what they're doing, and a great attitude. Think about it. Almost nine out of ten consumers will pay more for a great buying experience.

Then don't you owe it to yourself as a sales professional to have a great attitude every single day? W. Clement Stone once said, "There is very little difference in people, but that little difference makes a big difference. The little difference is the attitude. The big difference is whether it's positive or negative."

I'll never forget what I heard a speaker once say: "Every man is enthusiastic at times. Sometimes the enthusiasm lasts for 30 minutes, sometimes for 30 days, but the person who has it for 30 years is the one who's a very successful person." Being enthusiastic through the good times and through the tough times, having a winning attitude every time you see your prospects or your clients—that's what it takes to be a sales champion.

Ninety percent of your success in selling is your psychology. No matter what company you work for, no matter what you sell, there's always some form of sales training or sales planning. Getting yourself to do what you've planned and been trained to do is something different, and getting yourself to see things on a positive side is the most important part.

Once upon a time an optimist and a pessimist combined their resources and went into business together. Sales were great; they were fantastic! After the first three months, the optimist was really fired up. "What a great quarter!" he exclaimed. "Customers love our products, and we're selling more and more every week!" The pessimist answered, "Uh-oh. If things keep going like this, we're going to have to order more inventory." Everything that is happening in your day as a sales professional is a matter of perspective.

THE THREE LAWS OF ATTITUDE

So, here are what I call the Three Laws of Attitude:

1. *Attitude is a choice.* It's a choice. You're not able to control the weather, the interest rates, the stock market, or the traffic. Yet, every day that you wake up and put your feet on the floor, you can make a choice about how you're going to show up that day—how you're going to show up in front of your people, your clients, your coworkers. It's your choice.

2. *Your attitude alters your abilities.* When you make a decision to show up with a great attitude and full of enthusiasm, you tap into your true potential. How you think determines how you feel. How you feel determines what you do, and what you do determines what you get. When you have a great attitude, you are more, you do more, and you get more. Attitude alters your abilities.

3. *Your attitude affects the quality of your life.* This part of the book is focused on selling, yet we all do what we do for a quality of life. Having a great attitude has a direct impact on what you experience on a daily basis. The philosopher William James (1842–1910) said, "The greatest discovery of my generation is that human beings can alter their lives by altering their attitudes of mind."

So, let's put it all together. You're in the game of selling. You made the choice to be in one of the most rewarding professions in the world, where your job is to influence others to see the value of your product. Remember that people like to be around people who make them feel good, and people pay more for an enjoyable buying experience.

So here's your Action Plan for this chapter:

If you're not feeling great today, fake it! Or better yet, take a minute and reflect on all the things you can be thankful for, all the blessings you have, all the people who love and care about you, your health and your opportunities. With that in mind, make a decision to be someone others want to be around, someone positive, someone who sees the good in every situation.

You can do it. See yourself being successful, opening the account, reaping the rewards. Make it your personal challenge not to let outside influences affect your attitude. You're in control of your attitude. Maximize your attitude and maximize your income. Great job! Go out and take it to The Next Level!

CHAPTER 9

Get Rid of Your Excuses

Okay, I've got a question for you. You're in the game of selling, which is one of the highest-paid professions in the country, and if you're not getting the results you're looking for, what's your story? I mean, come on, you can tell me.

- ❑ Oh yeah, that's right, you've got the wrong territory.
- ❑ Oh, oh, yeah, I forgot, they changed your compensation plan.
- ❑ Whoa, whoa, wait a minute; your company doesn't do as much marketing and advertising as it should.
- ❑ Oh, yeah, yeah, that's right. You're in the tough part of the country right now.

Do any of these sound familiar? I hope not. I'm sure you've never used these excuses. I bet you know someone who has, though.

Since you've picked up this book, I'm making the assumption that you want the truth, the way you'd get it from a coach. A coach is different from a friend. A friend wants you to be happy, to feel good. That makes sense, right? Why would you want to have someone around you who makes you feel bad? So the friend will reassure you that you're still acceptable even though you're not getting what you want, and the friend will lend a sympathetic ear when you talk about how your company doesn't understand, or your boss doesn't get it.

A coach has a different purpose. I'm here to help you win, so I'm going to tell you the truth. Many of my clients tell me all the time that they value our relationship because they can talk to me about things they're not able to share at the office. Yet, more importantly, I'll tell them things that no one else will. It happens all the time in corporate America that high-level managers or execs won't give accurate feedback because they don't want to damage their relationship with the one on the other end.

So here's my coaching to you. If you want to take your sales to the next level, *you must get rid of your excuses.*

MONEY OR EXCUSES

Here's my motto that I use with my clients. I'm going to make certain you can remember these words. *You can make money or make excuses, but not both at the same time.*

So it's up to you. Which one do you want to make: excuses or money? Oh, gee, I'm sorry; I don't understand your situation because it's so unique. Is that right? Well, I'm not buying into that, because here's the reality: *At the end of the day, either you did it or you didn't.* The football player either caught the pass or didn't. The basketball player either made the shot or didn't. In the profession of selling, either you made the sale or you didn't.

You're making the required amount of calls, or you're not. You have a winning attitude, or you don't. You're preparing for your sales calls, or you're not. You've practiced overcoming objections, or you haven't. It's that simple. End of story. It's called eliminating your excuses and taking total responsibility for your results. You wanted the truth, right?

All my top clients are peak performers for a reason. They take personal responsibility for their results. It's no one else's fault. It's not the weather, the stock market, the interest rates, the competition. It's you. And the sooner you eliminate the excuses and move to complete responsibility, the sooner you enter the game with the top performers.

Excuses simply give us a reason to make us feel better about ourselves when we're not getting our results. They don't make us stronger, smarter, or more strategic. Excuses just help us feel less ashamed of ourselves. Meanwhile, the things we continue to excuse will return to haunt us over and over again.

How to Be a Real Loser

John Wooden was one of the greatest basketball coaches of all time. One of his principles was for his players to take full responsibility for their actions, both on and off the court. Wooden used to say, "No one's a real loser until he starts blaming someone else."

Let's face it—we all have excuses that seem real to us. "I mean, come on, it's not my fault. I would have hit President's Council last year, but one of my largest accounts didn't renew because of the economy." That type of thinking is a second-place mentality. That's right. You're shooting for second place, and that's not what we're looking for. I don't work with second-place people. My clients want to be the best. They want to learn more. They want to earn more. They want to be more.

Benjamin Franklin once said, "He who is good at making excuses is seldom good for anything else." No one's gotten successful making challenges or obstacles into excuses.

It's human nature that if you can find a reason to justify why you're not getting the results you want, you'll use it. There was once a farmer who asked his neighbor if he could borrow a rope, and the neighbor replied, "Sorry, I'm using the rope to tie up my milk." The farmer was stunned and he said, "You can't use a rope to tie up milk!" The neighbor responded, "I know that. But I don't want to do it, and that's as good an excuse as any." And so it goes for us as well—There's too much traffic, not enough prospects, too expensive. It's as good an excuse as any.

How to Become a Winner

Losers blame their circumstances; winners rise above.

- ❏ Colonel Harland Sanders was too old to start a business. Do you realize that he didn't start Kentucky Fried Chicken (KFC) till after he'd received his first Social Security check?
- ❏ Henry Ford faced a lack of demand for his automobiles. With his Model T, he made the market.

❏ Rudy Ruettiger, about whom I'll say more in the next chapter, became a football legend at Notre Dame in one play, though he had dyslexia and was considered too small to play football.

❏ Lance Armstrong had cancer. He won the world's most grueling bicycle race, the Tour de France, seven times.

❏ Donald Trump went bankrupt.

❏ The Wright Brothers knew that no one else had ever flown.

A young man once told Norman Vincent Peale that he wanted to start his own business but he didn't have any money. Peale told him, "Empty pockets never held anyone back. Only empty heads and empty hearts can do that."

A champion doesn't make excuses. Champions take full responsibility for their results. They commit to doing whatever it takes, whether it's staying late, making the extra call, having a winning attitude, or just plain old hard work.

Excuses are prevalent in our society and in all areas of life. How about in relationships? I hear this a lot: "Oh, I was traveling so much and we were so busy, and we just grew apart." That excuse is as good as any, yet it doesn't bring the advancement or improvement to the next relationship. It wasn't the travel or the business. The fact is, you didn't do the things necessary to have a long-lasting, loving relationship. You didn't do those special things. You didn't tell her how important she was to you. You didn't bring her flowers, look into her eyes, tell her you loved her. You didn't commit to doing what's necessary to build a relationship.

It's the same in selling. If you're not getting the results you want, there's no farther to look than in the mirror. The results you're getting are directly related to the things you're doing—or, more important, the things you're *not* doing. To be a champion you must be willing to do the things that others just won't do.

Jerry West, Hall of Fame NBA player and now general manager of the Memphis Grizzlies, once told me, *"Hard work will not guarantee your success, but without it you have no chance."* Are you making the number of calls necessary to be successful?

Are you prepared for each call? Are you returning your phone calls? Do you believe in your product or your company and your service? Do you have a winning attitude? So the step to really getting results is to get rid of your excuses. Make a decision today to play at The Next Level. As I've said, it's not the weather. It's not the marketplace. It's not the territory. It's not the pricing structure. It's you! And I mean that in a positive way. Because when it's you, you're able to make the adjustments and change your results.

Start today by getting rid of your excuses. You can either make money or make excuses, but not both at the same time. So when something doesn't go your way, rather than pointing your finger and looking for an out—look in the mirror. That way you have control and you can make changes. Let experience be your teacher and alter your procedure. Here's your Action Plan:

> *Start today with an excuse-free dialogue. If someone asks you, say, why you didn't hit your numbers for the month, respond with, "I just didn't make it happen."*

That's how a champion responds. No excuses. Great job! Go out and take it to The Next Level!

CHAPTER 10

Perseverance

How important is perseverance for you to be as successful as you want to be? Well, let me share with you that perseverance is something that will turn an ordinary salesperson into a sales superstar. You can have all the skills—prospecting, closing, uncovering needs—yet without perseverance you'll find only average success. You'll get only what I call "the low-hanging fruit." If you have incredible perseverance, on the other hand, you can just have average sales skills yet still be a top performer and a top money earner.

You're in the game of sales. You picked it, and hitting obstacles is part of the job description. It's how you persevere through the challenges that will make or break you as a salesperson. John D. Rockefeller once said, "I don't think there's any other quality so essential to success of any kind than the quality of perseverance. It overcomes almost anything."

So, are you going through some challenging times right now? Are you facing some obstacles in your business? Well, this is the time for you to show everyone what you're made of. It's time for you to show people who you really are. This is the time that precedes greatness.

WHERE THE RUBBER MEETS THE ROAD

Charles Goodyear purchased a rubber life preserver out of curiosity. He was told that rubber would be of great value if the cold weather didn't make it hard as stone and heat didn't turn it to liquid. He thought to himself, "Hmmm, I think I could find a solution to that." Well, experiment after experiment failed, and the money he put into research was lost. His last dollar was spent, and his family suffered for the necessities of life. Even his best friends thought he was crazy. Once a man inquired about where he might find Mr. Goodyear, and he was told, "If you see a man with a rubber cap, a rubber coat, rubber shoes, and a rubber purse with no money in it, that's Charles Goodyear."

Yet Goodyear wasn't crazy. For five years he battled obstacles and adversities that would have disheartened any man, yet his efforts finally paid off. Out of the obstacles, hardships, and setbacks, Charles Goodyear won. He turned failures into success, defeat into victory, and you ride on his work every day—all because of his persistence.

THE TEST QUESTION

When you're feeling like you've hit the wall, like there's nowhere to go, remember it's just a test for you. If you quit now, you're just creating a pattern for the future. What are you going to do next time you hit some obstacles? I mean, you've heard the old saying, "Quitters never win and winners never quit."

So, how do you know when you persevered enough? I'll tell you when: *When you achieve what you set out to do—that's when it's enough.* Do you want to lead your company in sales? Do you want to open up the largest account? Well, let's keep pushing:

❒ Chester Carlson worked on his idea for using static electricity to record light patterns and attempted to raise money for nearly ten years before he could find backers for his process, which has made every modern copier and laser printer possible.

❒ Vince Lombardi didn't become a head football coach till he was 47 years old.

❒ Coca-Cola sold only 400 bottles of Coke during its first year in business.

❒ Albert Einstein's Ph.D. dissertation was rejected, and he was told his work was irrelevant.

❏ Theodor Geisel's first children's book was rejected by twenty-seven publishers. Most people would probably have quit after, oh, twenty-three. The twenty-eighth publisher found it a seller, and Geisel, better known and loved as Dr. Seuss, died knowing that his perseverance had resulted in educating and entertaining millions of children.

So, how many times have you attempted to open up that evasive account? How many times?

TO THE GOLDEN DOME AND BEYOND

I want to tell you a story about a friend of mine of whom some of you have heard, and who, by perseverance, accomplished the unthinkable. His name is Daniel E. "Rudy" Ruettiger. If you weren't following college football in 1975, you would have heard of him if you had seen the movie *Rudy,* one of the best sports movies of all time. Rudy was an average football player in high school with below-average grades, yet his dream was to play football for Notre Dame. It was his perseverance that enabled him to do it.

First of all, he didn't have the grades to get into the university, let alone the football skills yet. He entered the associated junior college, Holy Cross College, at the age of 23. Tests showed that he was mildly dyslexic, so he buckled down and learned to study as he never had before, and he made it into Notre Dame after two years. At first the coaches thought he was too small to play, yet he did make it onto the "scout team"—the squad that the varsity practiced against. Rudy went to every practice and played as hard as if it were a real game. At last they let him suit up for the final game of his senior year. With less than half a minute to go, he was sent in for the first and only time. In that one play he sacked Georgia Tech's quarterback and saved the game for the Fighting Irish. Even thirty years later he remains the only player from Notre Dame to be carried off the field on his teammates' shoulders after a game.

The movie wasn't just about football; it was about perseverance. The story is amazing by itself. Yet the story that most people don't know that's just as amazing is how he got the movie made. Rudy graduated from Notre Dame when he was about 26 years old. He did a lot of things—ran a janitorial supply business, sold cars—and one day a guy told him he had a great story and he should write a movie. So he got excited and he wrote his story to the best of his ability, and he started asking around for producers. He moved to southern California, and, as he told me, he used to go into coffee shops and delis in Santa Monica and just look at people, wondering whether maybe they were producers. After years of obstacles, small successes, and more setbacks, he found a writer who was interested. Ah, but that didn't work out either. All the while Rudy's friends thought he was crazy, and they scoffed at his dreams.

Once when he was feeling a bit down and he was watching TV, he happened to catch Robert Schuller's *Hour of Power* show, and he heard the words "Tough times never last; tough people do" (which is the title of a book by Schuller). Rudy told me that on hearing those words he jumped up from the couch and shouted out loud, "Hey, I'm a tough guy! I can make this happen!" And he kept going.

Shortly after that, he met a guy who was a friend of a screenwriter named Angelo Pizzo, whose *Hoosiers* had been nominated for two Oscars and a Golden Globe, and he said, "Rudy, you need to tell your story to Angelo." Well, they set up a meeting at a local deli in Los Angeles, and Rudy showed up, excited—but Angelo wasn't there. Rudy went and stood outside the deli and saw the mailman come along. Rudy struck up a conversation, the mailman asked Rudy what he did for a living, and Rudy started telling him about football and Notre Dame and about how he'd written a movie and was waiting to meet this writer named Angelo Pizzo but he wasn't there. The mailman responded, "You mean you're looking for Angelo?" Rudy said, "Yeah! Yeah, I'm looking for Angelo but he's not here." The mailman replied, "Hey, I'm not supposed to tell you this . . . but he lives right over there." So Rudy walked over to Pizzo's house, rang the doorbell, introduced himself, and handed him the script. Even with that, there were still more obstacles along the way. Yet the bottom line is that the movie got made, starring Sean Astin (while Rudy himself appeared in it as a fan in the stands), and was an immediate hit. The movie led to Rudy visiting the Oval Office and meeting the President, and his life changed forever. Yet none of that would have happened without perseverance.

What's really funny about this story is that Rudy tells me he's not good at sales. Yet if you were a sales manager, wouldn't you love to have someone like Rudy on your team?

Rudy struggled for years to realize his dream. He told me he was broke till the movie came out, when he was 45. Now he's going around the country as a success story. He's a celebrity. Rudy and I live in the same neighborhood, and we both have young daughters who are similar in ages, so last Halloween our families went out trick-or-treating together. We knocked on some doors, and at one of them, out came Jason Giambi, the Yankees' first baseman and American League Comeback Player of the Year for 2005. As the kids yelled, "Trick or treat!" Jason said, "Hey Rudy! How you doin'?" Here was a baseball star who was excited to see Rudy, because anybody who's a success has total respect for what it takes to persevere through obstacles and adversity.

So, how about you? Are you willing to persevere through the tough times, through the times when things aren't going so well? Perseverance is a seed to greatness. So whatever you're experiencing right now, you can do it. Remember Schuller's motto: Tough times don't last; tough people do.

So, here's your Action Plan.

Make it a decision right now to keep going.

I mean, you have two choices: to quit or to keep going. If you absolutely knew that success was right around the corner, would you keep pushing? Would you keep going? Of course you would. So let's do it, because I can guarantee you one thing: If you quit now, there will be *no* success. Attack today with a renewed sense of confidence that everything is going to work out. You will be successful. Great job! Go out and take it to The Next Level!

CHAPTER 11

Phone Skills

So, I'm just curious. How many calls are you going to make today? Come on, you can tell me. Ten calls? Twenty calls? Fifty? More than 50?

Wait a minute. Are you going to tell me you're not sure, or you really don't have a number? That's a sure sign of under-performance.

Let me ask you a question. On a scale of zero to ten, ten being the highest, how much do you like making calls? If you answered anything less than an eight, we've got to talk.

Now let me get this straight. You've chosen sales as your means for making a living, one of the highest-paid professions in the country, and you don't like making calls? What if you knew that the more calls you made, the more money you'd make? Would that make a difference? I would think so, yet that's the way it is, and it has been so for years. The more calls you make, the more qualified prospects you'll find, the more meetings you'll set, the more presentations you give, and the more sales you'll make. That's a pretty simple formula, wouldn't you agree?

Even so, I've talked to many people across the country who use the term "call reluctance" as part of their vocabulary. Somehow, they think that phrase gives them the justification for not doing what they need to do to be successful in selling.

Let me give it to you straight. To be a top performer, a sales *professional*, you must—and I emphasize *must*—master the telephone. The fact of the matter is that you don't even have to be that good at it. Just getting yourself to *make* the calls will increase your qualified prospects. Take it to the next level and improve your phone skills, and you're unstoppable.

MAKING THE CALL

Let's talk about making the calls first. Are you making the calls you really should make to be successful in your business? Yes or no? You know the answer—I know you do. If the answer is no, let's talk about the psychology of the phone itself, actually getting you to a place where you can make the calls. I've said throughout this book that 90 percent of your success is psychology; it holds true here as well. Ninety percent of being successful on the phone is in your mind: simply getting yourself to dial the phone.

Previous clients of mine have told me about what they went through in the past before they made the shift in their mind. They would tell me about *thinking* about making the calls, but then finding other things to do instead so that they could put off making the calls. When they finally got themselves to sit in front of the phone with the intent of dialing, they imagined an angry person on the other end of the line, or they felt that they would be bothering someone or feared not saying the right thing. All of those thoughts led them to not dial the phone.

Here's the reality, as I've mentioned before: Half the things you believe aren't true anyway. So, if you're going to believe something, make it positive—make it something that'll get you some results.

Here's the belief of the top sales performers. They believe that the person they're about to call really, *really* needs their service, that the person can really use their help (perhaps having been jerked around by an amateur working for the competition). They also believe they bring real value to the client and that their product and service can improve the client's business and bottom line.

So, let me ask you the question. If you absolutely knew that the person you were going to call just had a real bad experience with a competitor's salesperson who led your client down the wrong path or was dishonest, and the client really wants to make a change but just doesn't know how or where to start, would you make the call? Yes or no? Well of course you would.

I know, I know, and I've heard this from the doubters before: "Well, what if it's not true?" Here's my response: "What if it is?" What if it is true and you *don't* call? Whom are you letting take your potential account? What if the client is really looking for someone, yet you don't make the call? Whom are you letting take your commission dollars? Whom are you allowing to take your son's or daughter's tuition or a downpayment on that vacation home when it could have been yours? The fact of the matter is that you *don't* know. You don't know that the person really wants to talk to you—just as you don't know that the person doesn't want to talk to you.

What separates the top professionals from the ones who struggle is that the top people *make the call*. What if you knew that you had a smiling customer at the other end, actually waiting for your call? Can you picture that? Picture your prospect sitting at the desk with a smiling face, waiting for a professional just like you to call. Put that picture in your mind before every call.

Or maybe it's the money that's going to drive you. What do you really want right now that you don't have? Is it a material item—a car, a boat, a new house, a flat-screen TV? Or else it's more time you're really looking for—a nice vacation, more freedom. Well, whatever drives you, you can have it *only* if you start making more calls today.

There's a four-step process for mastering the phone and making money. Here are the first three steps:

1. *Decide what you want that you don't have*—that car, that house, that boat, that wardrobe, or maybe a vacation or more time with your family. Whatever it is, create a picture in your head of doing or having what you really want. See yourself up on the beach or playing golf. See yourself coming home to the new house or driving the new car. See a picture and see yourself in that picture. Make it real. That's the first step.

2. *Understand that the phone will get you in that picture.* The phone is your tool to get you what you want. So, when you talk to yourself, you need to replace any negative language you have about the phone with language such as "The phone makes me money" or "When I dial the phone I'm one step closer to getting what I want"— something like that. That needs to be your new mantra, something positive.

3. *Imagine the person you're about to call as someone who really wants to hear from you.* They need you. They want you and you can help 'em.

MAKING THE CALL GREAT

Now it's time to talk about Step 4, and it can make or break your call. I'm not going to give you any phone skills training here, because there's so many ways to succeed on the phone; there are many different philosophies and different styles.

Yet here's what I want you to know: There's one way I will guarantee you will *not* succeed. That's talking to your prospect as if you've just lost your best friend, as if you really need *your prospect's* help because you're in such a slump. That will make Steps 1 through 3 totally irrelevant. You've got to bring some juice, some fire, some excitement!

Let me be very clear: Selling is nothing more than a transfer of feelings and a transfer of emotion, and *you cannot give what you don't have.* So, get excited! Get some energy in your voice! Stand up from behind your desk. Or, if you're in your car, imagine that you're standing.

When I say "bring some energy," I mean do it in an appropriate manner. Just be upbeat. Be positive. Be a problem solver. Don't be manic. You know what I mean, right? You've heard that person before:

(Level 20 energy) "Hey, how ya doin? I'm doing great!! Wow!!! I'm so excited!! I don't know what I'm excited about!!! Hey!!!!"

That's not the guy you want to talk to. That's not the person you want. Just have some fire. Be someone the customer wants to be around.

So, let's review, and let this be your Action Plan for this chapter:

> *Step 1: Decide what you want that you don't have, and picture yourself having it.*
> *Step 2: Understand that the phone will get you in that picture.*
> *Step 3: Image the person you're about to call as someone who really wants to hear from you.*
> *Step 4: Bring some fire, baby! Have some fun. Bring some energy when you are making the call.*

Have some fun. Bring some excitement to the table! Great job! Make your phone your friend and take it to The Next Level!

CHAPTER 12

Increasing Your Performance

So, let me ask you a question. How do you increase your performance from where you are now to where you want to go?

My experience, in working with the top sales performers, is that if you do what you're supposed to do—make your calls, make your follow-up calls, prepare properly, put together a great presentation, have obvious product knowledge, and, of course, ask for the order—you're going to be successful.

Yet, here's what I want you to know: the highest-paid sales professionals in the country—the people who are really making it happen—are not the smartest people around, the best dressed, the most articulate, or the best looking. They're not! They're simply the people getting themselves to do the little things day after day after day. They get themselves to take action and follow through.

NO MAN'S LAND AND THE SHOULD ZONE

Here's what I know about the sales professionals: When I find people who aren't getting the results they're looking for, what's often going on is that they get in the place I call *no man's land*.

No man's land is a place where you're really not happy about what's going on in your business. You're not hitting your numbers. You're not making the money you want to make. You don't have enough qualified prospects. You're not closing enough. You're unhappy about all these aspects in your business, yet you're not unhappy enough to do anything about it.

So, what do you do? Well, my experience says you moan, you complain, you point fingers at why you're not doing so well. And then what happens is that you graduate from no man's land to another place, which I call *the should zone*. It's a natural progression. People go from no man's land to the should zone.

The should zone is where you're saying to yourself, "You know, I really should get serious about my business. I really should make phone calls every day. I really should have a great attitude. I should prepare better for my presentation. I really should understand my customers' needs. I should, I should, I should, and I should." And then, of course, you "should" all over yourself. "I should, I should."

COACHING FROM TONY ROBBINS

I remember having a conversation with Tony Robbins on his resort in Fiji. We were talking about business, life, goals, personal stuff, where I wanted to go in the next five years. We're sitting on his porch overlooking the Pacific Ocean and he asked me, "Dan, can I give you some coaching?" and I'm thinking to myself, "Is he kidding? This guy's *asking* me if he can *give* me some coaching?" To put it into perspective, when I left Tony in 1999, he had multiple clients paying him a million bucks a year for personal coaching. Now he was offering me some coaching? I was all over it, right? So he looked at me and he said, "Dan, if you want to get yourself to the next level, whether it be socially, emotionally, financially, or spiritually, you've got to get yourself to raise your standards." He was really intense about it, and I was thinking to myself, "Raise my standards? What does that mean?"

As if he had been reading my mind, he said, "Raising your standards is taking a couple of those 'shoulds'—you know, the things you really *should* do—and turning them into a *must*, something that you absolutely must do. That's how you raise your standards: turning your shoulds into musts."

As human beings, we do the shoulds when it's convenient. Have you ever known someone who's joined a health club with full intention of going to the gym three or four times a week and really getting in shape? You probably know someone like that, right? Going to the gym for most people is a should because they really *want* to get in shape. You've done that, right? "I really *want* to. I really *want* to make more money. I really *want* to be a top performer in my office. I really *want* to have a better relationship." Yet if the want remains a want, it's not going to happen.

Human beings rarely get what they want, yet they must get what they need. Shoulds are similar to wants, and musts are similar to needs. Wants are plasma TVs, a new BMW 7 Series, a new house, a new wardrobe. Those are wants. Needs are food, air, clothing, and water.

I hear it all the time. Whenever I'm doing a speaking engagement in January, it's great to see all the people with New Year's resolutions. I get a lot of people who will come up and share their goals with me after my presentation; many of those are fitness goals. I remember this one gentleman who came up to me in Chicago all jacked up, telling me, "This is my year, man! I'm dropping 15 pounds. I'm going to eat right. I'm going to get ripped!" He had the best intentions, and there are many people with those same feelings.

Then, of course, they have a long day at work, and they start saying to themselves, "Wow! What a day! I need to unwind a bit. I'm going to happy hour with my friends. I'll work out tomorrow." Then tomorrow comes around, and they think, "Hmm. Shoot, I'm not going to work out today, it's raining." Then the following day the line is "Huh, not working out today, it's sunny." And they keep shoulding. "I should, I should, I should." And they get the same results they had last year. You have to raise your standards by taking shoulds and turning them into musts.

HENRY THE WALKER

I remember one fall day in Michigan as I was getting ready to go to school, and a brisk wind was blowing the leaves around—great football weather. I looked out my window, and I saw Henry, one of our neighbors, walking around the neighborhood. He had this green/blue warm-up suit on and looked kind of silly, I thought. I remember saying to myself, "What's he doing walking around the neighborhood?" It was kind of uncharacteristic for him. I didn't pay much attention to it, yet the next day there he was walking again, and then again the next day.

From that brisk fall morning on, he walked every single day all through my junior and senior years. When I would visit home during college, there was Henry walking through the neighborhood.

Why do you think Henry made the decision to start walking and really stick to it? Well, as I found out, he'd had a heart attack. Now read this story very carefully. I want you to understand this concept. Henry was an intelligent man, and he'd really known that he *should* exercise because he had high cholesterol and high blood pressure. Yet when he had the heart attack, what happened to the should? That's right, it became a must! And he raised his standards.

So what about you? Do you want to exceed your quota, double your income, get a promotion? What is it that you want to do? I'm here to tell you that whatever it is, you can make it happen. You just have to raise your standards by taking shoulds and turning them into musts.

Now, I'm not asking you to turn your whole life around, just a couple of small changes. If you make a couple of changes today, change a couple of shoulds to musts, and stick with it, your life will never be the same.

So here's your Action Plan for this chapter:

Identify one should in your business, just one, and turn it into a must.

My goal is to help you make one small shift that will get you your results. For instance, "I should make an extra ten calls every day. I should build better relationships with my clients. I should prepare better for my meetings. I should plan my days the night before, or my weeks in advance. I should practice my closing skills with someone. I really should have a better attitude." So what's it going to be for you? Make it happen. Find one should and turn it to a must. Focus on it. Put it on a note card in your desk, on your mirror, in your car. Whatever you focus on, you get. So keep that new must in front of your face. Great job! Go take it to The Next Level!

CHAPTER 13

Preparation

If you're the quarterback of an NFL football team, how important is your preparation? You bet! It's very important. How about doctors or lawyers? Well, it's the same for them as well.

How about you, the sales professional? How much do you prepare before going into battle against your competition? And I know you've got competition; every sales professional does.

I'm going to share with you a concept I use with my clients, called IPO:

❑ Investing
❑ Practice
❑ Outcome

How I use it is simple. *Investing* plus *practice* will give you your desired *outcome*.

INVESTING

First, let's talk about investing. I'm not talking about investing your money in the stock market. I'm talking about investing in yourself—investing in you. I've seen many people struggle in sales and not understand they're missing the winning edge.

I once met a very successful man who shared with me his beliefs on investing in yourself. He said that investing in himself gave him a tenfold return on the investment: for every hour he invested in himself, he got ten hours in return; for every dollar he invested in himself, he received $10 in return.

How many years does a doctor go to school before earning the first dollar? Eight? Ten years, maybe, and hundreds of thousands of dollars? How about a lawyer? Pretty much the same: eight to ten years and hundreds of thousands of dollars.

What about a sales professional? How long does a sales professional have to go to school before earning that first buck? I think you get the picture. What's ironic about that is that selling is one of the top money-earning professions in the world, right behind athletes and entertainers. So I'm going to share with you what the top sales professionals do to invest in themselves, and you too can do it—immediately. I'm going to share with you three quick ways that high-performance sales professionals invest in themselves—very simple.

You're already doing one right now: *reading*. Top sales performers are always reading something to help their businesses or empower their minds. How about you? How often do you read something, either for your business or for your mind? According to *USA Today*, 54 percent of the people in our culture—over half the people you and I meet—have never, ever finished a nonfiction book after they completed high school, which is amazing. What's more, the average person in our country watches between three and five hours of television a day, and one in five still watches Jerry Springer. Now, I know you're not average, and you're not in that category, yet these statistics are eye opening. The flip side is that, as Brian Tracy says, "If you can get yourself to read ten nonfiction books a year, you'll put yourself in the top 5 percent of the country in regards to that specific knowledge area." What's the biggest hurdle in reading? Here's what I hear: "I don't have the time." So here's some coaching for you. If you're using time as an excuse not to read, here's a strategy that I call the *ten-minute kickoff*. Read ten minutes each morning before you leave for work. Just by reading for ten minutes, you'll find your mind is sharper. It's focused on the things that help you get better and keep you going. You might have heard the old "golden hour" story, meaning reading for an hour a day? Well, I don't know about you, but most of my clients don't have an hour a day to read—yet they all have ten minutes. You'll find ten minutes will help you build momentum and help you grow as a sales professional.

Here's the second strategy: *listening to training or motivational CDs*. If you're just not the reading type, information on prospecting, closing, relationship building, and overcoming objections is available on CDs. There are two reasons why people don't use this strategy. One is that they're always on the phone—and if you're on the phone closing business, I can accept that because that's the outcome you're looking for. But the other reason is that people would rather listen to the radio or musical CDs. I've got some experience here. Years ago, before I understood the power of investing in myself, I could get in my car anywhere in the country, turn on that radio, and know every lyric to every song. I never closed one deal or made one sale from knowing song lyrics. Just as with reading, if you apply the ten-minute strategy to empowering yourself in the car—say, just listening to one track from my *10 Minute Coach* each day—you'll feel stronger, gain momentum, make more sales, and make more money. Can you listen to something for ten minutes a day? Yes or no? Yes, of course you can! If I'd told you to listen to it for an hour, you might say, "No, I don't think so"—yet ten minutes a day you can do. If you listen to something positive for ten minutes a day for a week, that's close to an hour. After a year that's 52 hours of information going into your head on overcoming objections, prospecting, closing, relationship building. That's close to two university semesters. If you do nothing else but listen to something positive in your car for ten minutes a day, your business will change.

The third and final investment strategy is going to *live training events*, whether public seminars or private sessions. The top sales professionals are always exposing themselves to what's out there, learning new skills, and meeting new people. By the way, what type of people do you think go to these events? That's right: successful people—people looking to get better, the type of people you want to be around and network with. My suggestion is, do *at least* two live events per year, such as my *High Impact Presentation Training* or *Sales Mastery* courses.

That's a minimum. (Your company can book me for these events or visit www.danlier.com for more information.)

So that's it. The three investment strategies for preparation are reading informative material, listening to training or personal growth CDs, and going to live training events. These add up to the winning edge. Think of it as preparing for your competition. What if you aren't doing these things and your competition is? You're behind already! So sharpen your mind, empower yourself, and expose yourself to the leaders in their field to grab tools and increase you skills. So that's the I in the IPO: investing.

PRACTICE

The P in IPO is very simple: Practice. If you wanted to become a professional golfer, what would you need to do? Practice. If you wanted to go to the Olympics, what would you need to do? Of course: practice. And, as the cab driver answered when the singer asked how to get to Carnegie Hall—practice, practice, practice. Why should it be any different for you?

It's interesting to me—given that professional selling is one of the highest-paid professions in the world—that many people have never practiced until they started working with a coach.

I mean, are you kidding me? How can someone expect to rise above the competition by just winging it? It's kind of scary, because so many are people are doing it and they're even (moderately) successful. Imagine if they actually practiced!

Now, what do I mean by practice? Very simple: finding areas within your game of selling, so to speak, that you need to improve on, such as overcoming objections and closing. I think you'd agree that those skills are important in your being successful.

When a prospect tells you, "I don't have the time," "It's too expensive," or "I'm just starting to look around," how do you respond? Is it something you have to think about? If so, you're leaving money on the table. You need to practice until you don't have to think about the answer.

Even if you go to a training session or attend a sales mastery course, you still have to practice. You wouldn't expect to go to the gym once and say, "Hey, I'm in shape!" No, baby, it's repetition!

That's it. IPO: *investing* in yourself through reading, listening to training CDs, and going to live training events, and then *practicing* your skills. When you invest and practice as a professional, you will get the *outcome* you desire.

THE OUTCOME

So, here's your Action Plan:

> *Start investing today. Start reading a book that will improve your business and empower your mind; listen to CDs such as* The 10 Minute Coach *to keep you on track in your business; and go to a live training event at least twice a year. That's the easy part. Then you have to practice.*

If you want to become a professional in one of the highest-paid professions in the country, you must practice. Find someone in your office who's motivated just like you and do some role-playing. Work on it! Remember, successful people will do what the failures won't. If you really want to go to the next level, then practice. Get a coach who has a background in selling. Great job! Stay focused, practice, and take it to The Next Level!

The Success Mindset

Being an extraordinary sales professional requires an extraordinary mindset. As I have said in this book, and as I stress in all my live events, 90 percent of life is related to your psychology—your mindset. This chapter is about the foundation of a *success mindset*: your beliefs.

In order to reach the top of any sales organization, you must have a solid belief system. Suppose I were at a company's awards banquet honoring the top sales professional for the year and I asked that person, "What do you believe is going to happen next month?" I'd get a response something like this: "I'm going to lead the company in sales. I'm going to make 100 calls a day, overcome the objections, and build my relationships. I'm going to make it happen!" Top sales professionals just have the *belief* that they're the best and that no matter what circumstances, they're going to make it happen.

A belief is nothing more than a sense of certainty. And what we've found is that the most successful people are the ones who are most certain about what they're doing for a living, especially in the game of selling. When you meet top sales professionals, they have absolute certainty in three areas.

❏ They believe in themselves.
❏ They believe in their company.
❏ They believe in their products and services.

As a sales professional you're not going to reach the top by being uncertain in any of these three areas. Think about it. If you believe in yourself and you believe in your company, yet you don't really believe in the product, how effective are you going to be at creating value? Not very. If you believe in your company and you believe in what you're selling, yet you really don't believe in you, how will you do then? Well, you might do all right, yet you'll never be a top-tier sales professional. It's not possible.

You see, as a human being, you cannot get yourself to do something you don't believe is possible. It just won't happen. That's why it's very common to see a new salesperson open up a monster account: because they don't *know* any better. They didn't *know* that no one had been able to open that account for ten years. They didn't *know* that the account was too big or the competition had a lock on it, so they went after it. If you, on the other hand, as a seasoned sales professional, believe that you'll never get that big account, you won't even call on it. You won't even put them on your call list. You won't stop by, or you won't even send them a Christmas card, because if you don't believe it's possible, you won't do what's necessary to get it.

A belief is a sense of certainty, and whatever you believe is true and true for you only. If you believe you're a great sales professional, you'll walk with certainty and you'll walk with confidence. If you don't believe in yourself, you'll present yourself with uncertainty and give a weak presentation. In Chapter 1, I told a story about meeting a guy who was 26 years old and making over a quarter million dollars a year. As you may recall, I took him out to breakfast, picked this young guy's brain, because I wanted to find out what he was doing, and he proceeded to tell me I'd never earn $250,000.00 a year. "I don't care what you do or how hard you work," he said, "you're never going to earn that kind of money." You can imagine me sitting there, saying to myself, "Well, great! Thanks!" He saw my body language and said, "No, no, Dan. I really like you, but listen to me very carefully. You'll never earn $250,000 with that $110,000 belief system you currently have inside your head." And he was absolutely right. You'll never earn a quarter million dollars with a $100,000 belief system, just as you'll never earn $100,000 with a $50,000 belief system. You see, the fundamentals hold true no matter what the numbers are; you'll never earn \$1 million with a \$500,000 belief system. You'll never outearn or outsell your own belief systems. So the first step in taking your sales career to the next level is having a belief system that supports your vision.

So what are your beliefs? Do they propel you to greater heights? Or do they hold you back? Sales professionals who have not reached their true potential typically have beliefs that hold them back. I'll give you a couple of examples.

- ❐ "I don't have a good territory."
- ❐ "I'm not a good closer."
- ❐ "Our product is too expensive."
- ❐ "I don't have the resources."
- ❐ "I don't have the time."
- ❐ "I don't have the experience."

Do any of these sound familiar? Remember, beliefs drive your behavior. So, if your *belief* is that you don't have a good territory, you won't make enough calls or see enough prospects—because, of course, it's not a good territory. Why would you want to go out and do all that work in a territory that's not very good? And, of course, with that type of work procedure you'll get mediocre results, which support your belief that it's not a good territory.

On the other hand, here are a few beliefs that will support you in being a top-flight sales professional.

- ❐ "I am the No. 1 sales professional in the region"—or even "I'm the No. 1 sales professional in the country."
- ❐ "People always buy from me."
- ❐ "I always build relationships that lead to sales."
- ❐ "My clients respect my knowledge."
- ❐ "I earn \$250,000 (\$500,000, \$1 million) a year."
- ❐ "When I do what I'm supposed to do, I always exceed my quota."

Let's have some fun for a minute. If your belief was that "Everyone I meet wants to buy from me," then you'd make the extra call. You'd have a great attitude. You'd introduce yourself to people with confidence, because everyone you meet wants to buy.

Now, even if your belief *is* that everyone wants to buy from you, do you think that everyone you meet actually will buy from you? Well, no. Yet I guarantee you that you'll make more sales than someone who believes he's just an average sales profes- sional, because you'll make more calls, have more enthusiasm, and walk and talk with confidence. Because, remember, beliefs drive your behavior.

So let's identify one of your beliefs that's holding you back. What is it? I mean, what's the voice inside your head saying that's holding you back? "I'm not good enough. I'm not smart enough. I've never earned that much before. I don't have enough experience." I mean, what is it? The first step is to identify your negative or disempowering belief. What is your disempowering belief? To be an outstanding sales professional you must change the disempowering or negative belief to an empowering belief, which is a belief that propels you.

A strategy you can use right now to get a jump on it is called the "as if strategy": Simply acting *as if* you were the top sales professional in the country. I've talked more about this strategy in Chapter 2.

So if you believe, throw away your doubts, fears, and self- imposed limitations, because once you believe, whether it's true or not, you'll act as if it is.

If you were the top sales performer, what would you do today? Whom would you call? How would you walk? How would you talk? How would you plan your day? I mean, if you were the top sales professional in your company, how patient would you be? What kind of attitude would you have? How would you treat people?

So, your Action Plan for the day—just for today only, because I wouldn't want to make you too successful too quickly—just for today is:

Act As If.

Act as if you're the top sales professional in your company. *Act as if* you're the best at building relationships. *Act as if* you're the best prospector. Because if you were the best, what would you do? Great job! Go out and take it to The Next Level!

PART 3
Parenthood at the Next Level

CHAPTER 15

Raising Champions

I take a lot of pride in being a father, and not just an OK father but an extraordinary father. I am passionate about providing my children with a foundation that will give them the best chance to succeed at whatever they choose to pursue. My wife, Tammy, and I are focused on not just "raising kids" but developing leaders, raising champions. That's what it's really all about.

Let me ask you a question: As a parent, if you could wave a magic wand, what would you use it to create for your kids? Success? Happiness? Wealth? All of the above? There's nothing wrong with any of them—success, happiness, and wealth. Yet, if you want your children to have all those three, or even any one of them, they must, and I repeat *must*, have the tools to create those things for themselves. No one can make them successful except themselves. No one can make them happy except themselves. And no one can make them wealthy except themselves. Well, that last sentence isn't exactly true, because many kids inherit wealth. Yet that doesn't give them the ability to be successful. I've met so many people who are wealthy who are miserable, have low self-esteem, or both, because they never developed the habits, skills, and characteristics of a champion.

Tammy and I have two children, ten and eight, and both of us have worked with, mentored, and coached young kids, teenagers, and college students. These chapters contain specific tools to develop leaders, laying the foundation that will allow kids to be successful. So make a commitment to give your children the edge by applying what you read in this book, even if it's just one chapter a day, because over time you'll shift your mindset and alter the destiny of your kids.

LEADERS, FOLLOWERS, AND BELIEFS

The first day Tammy found out she was pregnant, we knew with 100 percent certainty what kind of child we were going to raise: a leader, a champion, a winner. When you look at people in general, not just children, there are typically what I call leaders and followers. Now there are many types of leaders: charismatic leaders, quiet leaders, vociferous leaders, yet they're leaders. They influence others with their certainty, and they get things done.

In order to raise a leader, or what I call a champion, you must instill three things:

1. A winning belief system
2. Healthy self-confidence
3. High self-esteem

As you remember from Chapter 1, a belief is a sense of certainty. Throughout my years of coaching I have found that the people who have the winning belief systems are more successful, more secure, and more self-confident than others who don't. The interesting part of the equation is that many of you reading this book right now are carrying around beliefs, which you acquired from your parents, which may be holding you back.

Here's what I mean. A friend of mind brought a friend of hers to one of my events in Los Angeles a few years back. This was a public seminar, meaning that the public could buy tickets to it, rather than a company booking the event for its own employees only. When we all went to lunch that afternoon, the woman was sharing with us that she was having a difficult time "breaking through"—if you will, taking her life and her income to the next level. I asked her a series of questions about what she thought was holding her back. She said she didn't feel as if she was "good enough" or "deserved" to have success in her life. I have heard the same kind of responses from many others over the years. "I'm not good enough. I'm not smart enough. I'm not good around people. I'm too tall. I'm too short."

I think you get the idea. These are called *disempowering* beliefs—beliefs that hold us back. The challenge is that people get these beliefs from the ones they love the most: their parents or other family members. You've heard parents who make comments to their kids: "Oh, you're clumsy. Oh, you're slow. You're never going to amount to anything. Oh, you're lucky to have that. Shut your mouth around adults. Children were meant to be seen and not heard." Well, inside the kids' heads those comments develop into beliefs that literally chart the course for the child's life.

POSITIVE PROGRAMMING

So here's the strategy we've used to build our children's belief system and self-confidence. It's called *positive programming*. Positive programming is simply giving your child positive feedback and literally programming the child for success.

When our kids were very young we did it all the time, and I mean all the time. For example, when our son was just a baby, I would talk to him and tell him how healthy he was, how smart he was, how handsome he was. It was just part of my conversation with him. Understand, at this point he didn't even understand me—although now I believe he did, unconsciously. And of course, we did the same thing for our daughter. When they ate their meal, Tammy and I would say, "Wow! You're such a great eater! You really like to eat foods that are good for you." And when we were around other people, I'd say, "Wow! You're really great around people. You have great manners. Mommy and Daddy are proud of you." And when we went to the pool, even before they could swim, I used to tell our son how great he was in the water, what a great swimmer he was.

Now, they're a bit older, so our programming is now a bit more focused. We tell them what great manners they have, and they've been told that for so long now that they believe it. They believe that they have great manners to go to the restaurant.

So, guess what kind of behavior they exhibit when they go to the restaurant? That's right; they always act appropriately at a restaurant. We tell them things like, "Wow, you're really smart for a second grader! You're amazing. You really have a creative brain. You'll probably invent something that will help people all over the world." We tell them how healthy they are and how their brain loves when they eat carrots and peas. We simply inundate them with positivity.

Now, let's keep it real here. I've heard some old-school parents telling me how that's not how the world is, or how kids are, and my response is this: "Exactly." Kids have the opportunity to encounter so much negativity and self-doubt that what a parent can do is build the foundation for success by building their belief system. Think about it. If you were told that you were smart, amazing, and could do and be anything you wanted in your life, and you were filled with encouragement and positive programming as a child, where do you think you'd be right now? Kids get enough negativity from others. They don't need it from their parents, too. Now let me be very clear. Do not mistake positive programming for a lack of discipline—two entirely different subjects here. Make no mistake: When our kids get out of line, so to speak, they encounter consequences; that's a must.

So, positive programming does two things that lead to building a champion. First, it gives a child an empowering belief system. An empowering belief system is a belief that enables you to go to higher heights. "I am strong. I am confident. I'm a leader. I'm great around people. I'm creative. I can do anything." Second, positive programming builds self-confidence. When you hear your parents telling you things that are positive, it builds your self-confidence. Self-confidence has a huge impact on a child's life. Kids with healthy self-confidence don't get involved with the wrong crowd, because they're not craving acceptance. They have it already. Kids with healthy self-confidence typically don't engage in troubled activities such as vandalism, shoplifting, or drugs, because they know they can meet the world head-on and don't have to lash out at it or numb themselves to it. Building self-confidence in your child will pay big dividends for you down the road.

HONEST SELF-ESTEEM

As I said earlier, the third characteristic of a champion is high self-esteem. Now, wow, here's a good one. How do you build self-esteem? Here's how—and if you're taking notes, write this one down.

Self-esteem is built by doing or completing things that are difficult or that you don't want to do.

The reason that there are so many kids running around with low self-esteem is that someone's always there to bail them out, to pardon them, to take the load off—thus robbing them of a reference for what's possible for themselves. I can remember that, as a kid, I was always having to do something I didn't want to do—cutting a cord of wood, running a mile, or completing a book report or a science project or my work around the house. I can vividly remember times that I really didn't want to do it, yet my parents made sure I completed the project or task, and it gave me a reference for what was possible for myself. They gave me the opportunity to build my self-esteem.

So, here's your two-part Action Plan for this chapter.

First, start building your children's belief system now. Tell them that they're strong, that they're confident and they have great manners, and people love to meet them. Do it tomorrow and do it again consistently. Write yourself a note to remind you that you're responsible for building an empowering belief system for your child.

Second, think about giving them the necessary self-esteem for being successful, by allowing them to have to push through things that they don't want to do. Refrain from coming to their rescue for every little thing that they encounter, or that challenges them. Build the muscle that will allow them to push through challenges that they encounter in their lives. That's the biggest gift you can give them.

Great job! Let's take this to The Next Level!

CHAPTER 16

Principles for Winning

When you talk with successful people, you'll find they have various principles for success that govern how they operate. With that in mind, my wife, Tammy, and I are proactive in the sense of teaching our kids these principles at a young age—principles that will make them winners in life. Here are a few that our son and daughter understand.

IF YOU WANT TO GET BETTER, YOU MUST PRACTICE

We've all heard that "practice makes perfect." Tammy and I say, however, "If you want to get better, you must practice." When we introduce our kids to new sports, I always practice with them to give them the edge, because I know what it takes to be successful in sports, which is what it takes to be successful in life in general. We've ingrained this in their heads. Now they'll come to me and say, "Daddy, I need to practice."

Our son played soccer when he was younger. Once his coach told him he was going to be the goalie for the first half of the next game, and he told me, "Daddy, I'm not really good at kicking like a goalie," which is similar to a punt in American football. So, I said, "Daniel, OK, what do we need to do?" He said, of course, "Practice."

WINNERS NEVER QUIT AND
QUITTERS NEVER WIN

This is a great motto in life in general. I mean, how many peo-ple have you seen who quit when times get tough? That's just not the answer, baby. Winners never quit and quitters never win.

HEALTHY FOOD EQUALS A HEALTHY BODY

We teach this: "If you want a healthy body, you must eat healthy food." When our kids aren't feeling great or are not feeling their best, we say, "Let's put some good food in our body. Let's eat some vegetables and carrots and peas. Let's eat some chicken." They understand that if they want a healthy body, they need to eat healthy food. It's a great success principle.

THE ONLY WAY YOU CAN FAIL IS
BY NOT GIVING IT YOUR BEST

I love this one. I believe it's important to teach our kids that it's okay not always to succeed—that is, we're not always going to win. Yet it's not okay not to give your best.

If their team loses a soccer game or baseball game, we always ask them, "Did you do your best?" Of course, they say, "Yes." It's not okay to lose because you didn't give it your all. That's a recipe for mediocrity. They always need to do their best. The only way you can fail in life is by not giving your best.

HARD WORK MAKES UP FOR
A LOT OF MISTAKES

Oh, man, I love this one as well. This is a philosophy that I use in my own life. I've seen so many winners in my life who didn't have the skills, yet made up for it with hard work and hustle. I've seen it in sports. I've seen it in business. I've seen it with kids. I've seen it in my life. There have been so many times in my life when I really didn't know how to get done what I had to get done. Maybe I was overmatched. Yet because of my hustle and work ethic, I came out on top.

So that's what we talk about with our kids. When you're going into a new experience, whether it's sports, business, life, whatever you're going to do, hard work will make up for a lot of mistakes. The reason is that there are always going to be other people who are better than you at it, but most of them are not willing to work as hard as you. So that's a great belief to have. It's a great principle.

YOU CAN HAVE ANYTHING YOU WANT IN LIFE IF YOU'RE WILLING TO PAY THE PRICE

This is simple. We want our kids to know that they can create anything they want, yet they have to pay the price. The price is discipline. The price is focus. The price is hard work. The price is overcoming adversity. I point out that they can do, be, and have anything they want in their life if they're willing to pay the price, because most people in life aren't. Most people want to be millionaires. Most people want to go here, want to go there. But they're not willing to do the things necessary to make it happen.

So our kids have to understand the principle that they can have anything they want in their life if they're willing to pay the price—doing the homework, being disciplined, cleaning their room, filling out their homework chart, showing persistence, or whatever it is they need to do. If they're willing to do those things, they can have and get anything they want, which is a great principle.

THE ONLY THING THAT LIMITS PEOPLE IS THEIR OWN MINDS

This is the last one, and one of the most important ones to me. I've seen so many people who are not getting the things they want in their life because of their belief systems, their negative thought patterns, their beliefs about the world.

So we teach our kids, "you can have anything you want. The only thing that limits you is what's going on inside of your mind." We see homeless people or people who are under-achieving, and we talk about how their minds are not healthy;

they have limitations in their minds that cause them not to reach their goals. So when we talk to our kids, we talk about understanding that they can do, have, and be anything they want. They have to believe it. They have to take action. They have to be positive, and they have to have a great work ethic, and that's the bottom line.

So, here's your Action Plan for this chapter.

In your home, talk about principles for winning. Implement some. Talk about them. Put them on your refrigerator. Talk to your kids about them.

Talk about whatever it takes to win so that they start having these principles as mottos inside their heads. When they go out into the real world and things get tough, they'll say to themselves, "Winners never quit and quitters never win," or "I can be and do and have anything I want if I'm willing to pay the price." That's valuable stuff. Those are principles for winning. Great job! Take it to The Next Level!

CHAPTER 17

Success Programming

You may have heard the old saying that you are who you hang around with. That could be scary for some of you. I remember that the first time I heard that phrase, I had to lose a few friends, if you know what I mean. Yet, quite frankly, who you are as a person has a profound effect on your kids.

Not all of us are always the most upbeat people in the world. That's OK. You don't have to be a motivational speaker to have a profound, positive impact on your kids.

Once, years ago, as I was on my way out to my car at a mall, I saw this woman in the parking lot, just verbally abusing her son, who I'd say was about three or four years old. I'm very sensitive to that, because there was a time in my childhood when I wasn't very popular, so I understand the impact of words on a child's psychology and self-esteem. She kept on telling her son that he couldn't do anything right and he was no good. I walked up to her—and, in retrospect, I probably scared her to death, because I'm 6 foot 8—and I said, "Excuse me." I said, "Your son looks like a great kid, and I know you don't mean what you're saying, but please, lady, don't take out your issues or frustrations on your son; they belong to you." And obviously, it was an uncomfortable moment for her as she quietly, with embarrassment, got into her car and drove off. Typically I keep my nose out of others' business, yet this lady was just over the line.

I'm sharing that story with you because you have the opportunity to program your child for success or for failure. I mean, think about it. If you keep your mind focused on something positive—say, if you listen to just one track of *The 10 Minute Coach* a day—you'll take actions that will enable you to improve. The same concept holds true for kids. They are so fragile. They can be programmed to be leaders, champions, and overachievers, or they can be programmed to be underachievers.

You're saying, "Wow, that sounds kind of intense." Well, it is to me. Tammy and I make it a responsibility to arm our children with the belief system they need to be successful under any circumstances, and, honestly, it's not that tough. You just have to be consistently positive—to "catch them doing things right," which, quite frankly, is in opposition to how our culture is programmed.

CATCHING THEM DOING IT RIGHT

Many parents don't give their kids feedback until they do something wrong. Well, that's very limiting. Imagine hearing things like "You never do anything right. You're driving me crazy. You're out of control. You're going to get in trouble. You're a bad boy," and on and on. Trust me, if you keep telling your son that he's a bad boy, guess what you're going to get? That's right, either a kid who's tuned you out, or a rebel who lives down to everything you've told him. You've created a label for him.

Now on the other hand, how about labeling your child in a positive manner: "You're amazing! You can do anything! You're so smart; you always do the right thing! You're a great baseball player! You're a great athlete! People love to be around you!" Imagine growing up hearing things like that.

Now I'm certain that wasn't the case for most of you. I know it wasn't for me. Not that my childhood was bad by any means. I mean, I turned out okay as far as I know. Yet, there's another level to develop a champion. So, first things first. Catch your children doing things right and get good at recognizing it. Overdo it. Build their confidence and self-esteem. Tammy and I are big on confidence, because I know that with confidence you can achieve anything in this world. So we're always telling our son and daughter how confident they are. I'll give you an example. Before we meet new people, we tell them in advance whom they're going to meet and instruct them to shake their hand and introduce themselves. Then, of course, we follow up by telling them how confident they are, to continue to build their self-esteem, self-confidence, and belief system.

Years ago, when my son was about four, we were at a park, and he was playing on the playground, sliding down the slide. A few other kids came over to the slide area. One girl was a bit older than him, maybe five or so, and I told him to go over and shake her hand and introduce himself. So, I watched him—of course, looking for another opportunity to tell him that he was amazing. He went up to her and he introduced himself and asked "What's your name?" The little girl didn't respond, she just kind of looked at the ground. After standing there for a couple of seconds, he came back over to me, and I asked, "Hey, what happened?" He answered, "Daddy, she just needs some more self-confidence," and I gave him a high-five and I told him he was amazing. The power of positive feedback—this is a very simple example.

Here are a few more very simple, fundamental examples to stir your thought processes. These are the kinds of things that our kids hear on a daily basis. When they brush their teeth, we say, "Wow, you do a great job brushing your teeth. You have amazing teeth. You always keep them clean." When they eat dinner, we say, "You're healthy. Your body loves those vegetables, they make you so smart." When we take them to restaurants, we say, "You really had good manners in the restaurant. You made Mommy and Daddy proud. We believe we can take you anywhere. Is that true?" And, of course, they respond with "Yes." "You're smart." "You're confident." "You're handsome." "You're really good at figuring things out." "You have a great imagination." "People like to be around you because you're so confident."

Now, understand, we don't overplay this stuff. These are just comments we make in passing, on the same level as the news— "Hey, it's sunny and 75 today," or "The Cubs won last night."

What has happened in our case is that our kids are so confident that they're not looking for approval from other kids to get their self-esteem. They already have it. Nor are they the kind of kids who say, "Hey, Daddy, Mommy, watch me! Watch me! Watch me!" When I see kids asking their mom or dad to watch them, I know they're not getting enough positive feedback at home.

PREPROGRAMMING

Now the next level here is what I call "preprogramming," or "future pacing," which simply means we tell the children in advance what's going to happen. For example, when they both were younger, before we went to a restaurant, we would tell them how great they were going to be at the restaurant. It would go something like this: "Now, when we go to the restaurant we always have great manners. Daddy and Mommy love taking you two to the restaurant because you're so good in the restaurant. When we sit down, Mommy has some paper and some crayons for you to do some drawing and be creative, and when we talk you use the kind of "restaurant voice," you know? That's right. And you guys have such great manners. So, do you have any questions about the restaurant?" They'd say, "No, Daddy." "OK, let's go."

What just happened is that I told them everything that was going to happen in the restaurant. I programmed them for success. Then of course, when we came out they got positive feedback for their behavior.

If we were going into the grocery store, before we walked in, I'd say, "I really like how you guys help me push the cart and find the groceries. You always have great manners in the grocery store." If necessary, I might break it down even more. For instance, "Now, before we go into the store, I have a quiz for you. Which is the type of behavior is appropriate for a grocery store? Running around and yelling, or walking with Daddy?" Of course, they'd say, "Walking with Daddy," and I'd respond by saying, "Wow, how'd you both get so smart? I love how you both have great manners in the store." So when we walked in, they'd already be programmed for success.

I've been through numerous levels of hypnosis training, and this is actually a hypnosis tool, but I don't use that weird hypnotic voice. This is a tool that master sales professionals use when selling their product or service. Ladies, have you ever heard something like this? "When you put on the dress you're going to notice the feeling of the high-quality fabric against your skin and how it makes you look two sizes smaller." Anyway, take it for what it's worth and "preframe" your kids on what's going to happen before it actually does. It takes a little practice, but it's fun and it works.

SUBCONSCIOUS PROGRAMMING

The last strategy I'm going to share with you is called "subconscious programming." This is a tool that Tammy and I have used for years. It's literally to program your kids for success subconsciously.

Now it sounds kind of freaky, I know, but let me give you a simple example. Medical students and law students use something called *accelerated learning* to help them learn better. They play Baroque music while they're studying, and it helps their synapses and neurons actually connect and they learn more effectively. I wish I would have been on that when I was going to school. So Tammy and I created a CD to help our kids build their self-esteem. It has our voices on it, saying, "You are strong. You are confident. You're a leader. You eat your vegetables. You sleep through the night"—which was important when they were young. It has some subconscious, nice, relaxing music in the background that builds their self-esteem and self-confidence. We call this *Subconscious Success Programming* (SSP). You can order your Subconscious Success Programming for Children CD at www.danlier.com.

So here's your Action Plan:

Catch your kids doing things right today. Tell them they're amazing, they're responsible, and they can do anything. And get good at doing it over and over.

Wow! What a great environment to grow up in. And then, use the preframe strategy and walk them through their success in their mind before they actually do it. Great job! Take it to The Next Level!

CHAPTER 18

Language

I am very passionate about this chapter, because as a success coach, I can tell a lot about people by the language patterns they use. I can tell what their beliefs are, if they are committed, and if they have the persistence to achieve their goals. This chapter is focused on the type of language you use with your kids.

I'm talking about some elementary language patterns that all of you know, yet many don't know the impact they have on development. In particular, I'll discuss three words that are not used in our house and are not a part of our kids' vocabulary. They are debilitating words—words that disempower kids and limit development. Well, living in our house with two success coaches for parents may be a little bit out of the ordinary, yet we're talking about raising champions.

This is a hot topic for me. I'm very passionate about it because language has a profound effect on behavior. I have a certification in Neuro Linguistic Programming (NLP), which is a fancy technical term for using language to affect behavior. NLP is most commonly used by therapists in dealing with changing behavior or overcoming addictions. As a coach, I teach these same principles to executives, yet the impact on a child's development can be just as empowering or debilitating.

CAN'T

The first word is "can't." "Can't" is a four-letter word in our house. Tammy and I don't use it and as our kids were growing up they never heard it, so, of course, they don't use it.

The power in this is that the word "can't" is overused by parents in communicating with their kids, and kids develop a belief that they have limitations on what they can achieve.

As a parent, I'm very involved with my kids. We do things together. I spend a lot of time with them. When their friends and classmates and their parents are around, I hear how other parents talk to their kids—through the ears of a parent and success coach. It's very common to hear things like, "Oh, you can't do this. You can't do that. We can't have this. We can't afford that. You can't. You can't. You can't. You can't!"

The challenge with this is that when many people hear the word "can't" even as adults, their brain immediately turns off, because they've been programmed to understand that "can't" means "it's not going to happen." So fast-forward into the future of your child. They're working on a new project, a new sport, a new hobby, and they're having a few challenges. Guess what they start to tell themselves? That's right. "I can't do this," which immediately shuts off the brain from working it out because they've been programmed since they were little kids that "can't" means "no," or "it's not going to happen."

Over the years I've done an exercise at my one-day events on taking your business or your life to the next level, which is called the nine-dot exercise. In case you haven't seen this exercise before, I ask my audience to draw nine dots on their paper; three lines of three, and I tell them the task is to connect all nine dots with four lines without lifting their pencil from the paper. If you've seen it before, bear with me. After about 30 seconds into the exercise, I tell the audience, "It can't be done, It actually takes five lines, and I made a mistake." What happens is that they immediately put down their pencils and look for more instruction. The fact is that it can be done. Yet, as soon as they hear the word "can't" they immediately stop, just as many kids do in life when they confront an obstacle or hear from someone that they "can't" do that. So instead of "can't," we use the words "not able."

Now, I know it sounds a little awkward, yet here is the distinction. The words "not able" do not have the finality, if you will, that the word "can't" has; they suggest that the inability is temporary. If my son were to ask, "Hey Daddy, can we go to Legoland tomorrow?" I'd answer, "Well, we're not able to go tomorrow, yet maybe sometime soon we'll make it happen." Tammy and I have used this language pattern since the kids were born, and now it's just a normal part of our language. When my son was five, I was doing a presentation on success principles in a hotel ballroom in central California for about 200 college students, and I was talking about the power of language. My family happened to be there during this part of the event, and I was talking about how the word "can't" paralyzes your progress. I had my son come up to the front of the room, in front of the audience, and I said, "Will you please jump and touch the chandelier that's hanging from the ceiling?" Now remember, he was five years old at the time. So he jumps up, and of course, he's only about 15 feet short of his target, and I say, "Come on, champ! Jump higher. You can do it! Touch the chandelier!" He jumps again and, of course, he's "just a little bit" short of his target, and I brought the microphone down to him and he said, "Daddy, I'm not able to touch it, but maybe someday when I get bigger." The audience started laughing. I tell you, sometimes the best teachers are kids. I asked the audience what distinction they made from my son, and one student said, "His response was optimistic; like he wasn't able to do now, but yet maybe sometime he could," and I said, "Exactly." So get rid of your can'ts.

TRY

The next word we don't use in our house is "try." "Try" is a weak word. It's not a winning word, it's not a leadership word—it's a weak word.

Here's an example. Suppose you've been asked to come to a party or a get-together at someone's house, and you run into them at the store or you're talking on the phone, and they say, "Hey, are you coming over this Friday?" and you say, "Oh, I'll try." Well, if I were a betting man I'd put money on your not making it. "I'll try."

Here, let me give you a simple example. If you're in the car listening to a CD, *try* to turn up the volume. Go ahead and try. Give it a try! No, no, no, no, DON'T DO IT, just try. Try as hard as you can.

I think you get the point. Winners don't try, leaders don't try, champions don't try. They do. They do it. They get it done.

Again, this is strictly language. The challenge with using the word "try" is that any time you don't achieve something, whether it's a fitness goal, a health goal, a financial goal, or whatever, you can just say, "Oh, I tried," and it makes you feel better.

We don't try at our house. We do it. Now the substitute word, or language, can be a couple of things. We say, "Give it a shot," or "Give it a go. Give it your best," or "Just do it."

Just last night we went to the baseball field and I was pitching to my son. After about ten minutes, my daughter said, "Daddy, let me do it!" She didn't say "Let me try." She said, "Let me do it." It's just a word, yet the impact is huge. "Let me do it." She used to say, "Let me give it a go," which sounds kind of funny, but that's the language we taught at our house instead of the word "try."

Even at the dinner table we say, "Would you like a taste?" rather than "Would you like to try it?"

Here's the psychology behind that. It's just too easy to say, "I tried." When people say "I tried," it just makes it all OK because "I tried!"

Can you imagine me telling my wife, "Tammy, honey, well, I tried to be faithful." I can tell you right now, that's not going to work. "Oh I really tried." Trying doesn't get it done. In life, you either did it or you didn't—that's it. "I tried to be a good father. I tried to go to the gym. I tried to be faithful. I tried to be honest." I mean, come on, give me a break.

Tammy and I created this strategy while reading children's books to our kids when they were very young. We were amazed at how negative many children's books are. We created a learning system called LSL®, which stands for Language-Sensitive Learning®. Take a look at our website, www.danlier.com, to find out where to get books that are LSL certified.

QUIT

The final word I'll address in this chapter is "quit." "Quit" is a disempowering word, and we don't use it in our house. Our kids don't know "quit." Quitting is not an option. Quitters never win and winners never quit. If you believe in that philosophy, there's never a reason to use the word "quit."

In our house we don't quit anything; we just simply do something else. Have you ever played a board game that turns into a marathon session, and everyone's saying, "Geez, enough already"? The tendency is, for someone to say, "Hey, let's quit the game." Yet, instead of using the word "quit," we just say "Let's put the game away for now" or "Who's ready to do something else?" Remember, it's a small distinction, yet it has a huge impact.

A while ago one of my children's friends was visiting. They were playing hide and seek, and he was it. Being at home, my children knew all the good hiding spots, and he wasn't able to find them. And it wasn't long before Tammy and I heard him shout out, "I quit!" Now understand, he's only six, and that's not the end of the world. Yet, we're out to build champions, and as kids get older, they start to face obstacles and challenges. If "quit" is part of your language, it becomes really easy to say, "I quit." Remember, quitters never win and winners never quit.

I have a client who was a smoker, and last month he decided not to smoke. Not to "quit smoking," but just not to smoke. He became a non-smoker. It's that simple. He just chose to do something else than smoke, rather than quit.

So here's your Action Plan for this chapter.

Get rid of your can'ts, tries, and quits.

I know it's difficult. Believe me, I know, because it starts with you. This is not going to happen without a buy-in from all members of your household. You and your partner must make the shift in order to give your child the winning edge. So give it a shot. Do it! Make it happen! Do it for your kids. Get rid of your tries, quits, and cant's and give your child the language for success. Great job! Take it to The Next Level!

Health and Nutrition

I'll let you know up front that I'm not a nutritionist or a health educator, yet in this chapter I'll talk generally about the impact of health and nutrition on raising champions.

Playing college basketball and being around athletics my entire life, I've always been interested in whatever could improve my performance. I have a master's degree in physical education, which necessitates the understanding of nutrition and exercise on the human body. So I do have some basis for my message here. Yet, as I said, I'm not going to go scientific on you here.

These are the basics. First and foremost, let's talk about nutrition. What are your kids eating? That question really means, "what are you feeding them?" So again, this is really about you and how willing you are to give your child the best possible chance for success. If you read the papers and magazines, there are more children diagnosed with attention deficit disorder (ADD) or attention deficit-hyperactivity disorder (ADHD) than ever before. When I was growing up, there wasn't an ADHD. They've had to create another category to give our kids another reason for that behavior.

Now I understand there are some legitimate medical concerns, yet let's talk about the diet of our kids. It blows me away when I see four-, five-, six-, seven-year-olds, ten-year-olds drinking sodas or eating candy. I mean, come on. What positive result is going to happen from that? I've even seen kids drinking sodas from their sippy cups. My son is 10 and my daughter is eight. They've never had a soda and, quite frankly, they don't want one. They believe that sodas won't allow their bodies and brains to grow.

SUGAR

In our house we talk about the impact of sugar on the body. Our kids eat a candy bar on occasion and they love cookies. I mean, Tammy makes the best chocolate chip cookies on the planet. Yet, it's a reward or a special occasion. It's not just an everyday thing.

If you have young children, you know about the birthday parties that are nothing more than a big sugar fest. We let our kids know up front that if they want to have cake at the party, they need to eat their veggies before we go to the party. We have an understanding in the nutrition and what the body needs. Again, we're simply building success principles at a young age.

How about a breakfast cereal? This is kind of fun to me. Can you believe the cereal aisle at the grocery store? It looks like a candy aisle: Fruit Loops, Lucky Charms, Frosted Flakes. Or how about the Pop-Tarts, you know, Frosted Brown Sugar Cinnamon. Wow! What a great breakfast. That's like a toasted candy bar. And we wonder why our kids have a challenge focusing at school.

I mean, come on, parents, let's get real. What Tammy and I have done is set a bar on their grams of sugar. Tammy typically fixes oatmeal or Cream of Wheat, yet we do have cereal, and the sweetest cereal we allow is Honey Nut Cheerios, and that's where we set the bar. We educated out kids on grams of sugar per serving and the impact of sugar on their bodies. So when our kids walk through the cereal aisle and they want to buy the latest, greatest, sugar-rich marketing fad, I tell them to check the grams of sugar. It's easy; they know the rules. If it has less than Honey Nut Cheerios, then we can get it. If it has more, it's off base.

SNACKS

How about snacks? From the start, we've always had fresh fruits or vegetables, so for a snack they'll eat apple slices, oranges, pears, peaches, even baby carrots with ranch dressing.

The challenge for this conversation is that kids really don't know any better. They don't understand nutrition, so if you eat poorly, there's a good chance your kids are going to eat poorly. It really makes me sad when I see young kids who have a weight challenge and I look at their parents and they're buying them pizzas, hamburgers, fries, Cokes.

Man, let me talk straight here. In all my years of coaching I've never met anyone who said, "You know, Dan, I'd really like to put on some extra fat this year." Because of the sheer numbers, there's a good chance that many of you reading this chapter have a few extra pounds you'd like to shed. This message really isn't directed at you or your body—it's your choice—but give your kids a chance. If you're eating poorly, there's a good chance your kids aren't eating well, which means they really don't have a choice.

EXERCISE

How about exercise? I mean, you've heard the numbers. Depending on what publication you've read, close to 60 percent of Americans are overweight or even obese, and we have a real challenge with obesity in children. Proper nutrition is one part; exercise is the other.

Note to parents of young kids: Refrain from buying electronic games such as PlayStations and GameBoys. Are you kidding me? Many kids today would rather sit and play with these gadgets for hours, which develops habits that lead to a sedentary lifestyle. Our kids think it's really great when they go to a friend's house and they get to play on a PlayStation. It's a treat for them. If you have the games already, put a limit on their use, or create a reward system to develop good eating and exercise habits and use the games as rewards.

Get your kids involved in sports or other physical activities. I'm a big believer in sports for many reasons, and health is one of them. If your kids aren't in sports, put together some kind of a weekly incentive program to earn allowance or a special toy they really want. How about riding bikes, inline roller-skating, skateboarding, rock climbing, even walking around neighborhood—there are so many things kids can do to increase their physical condition and build healthy bodies.

So here's your Action Plan in regard to health and nutrition:

Make a decision about what you really want for your kids. If you want them to be their best and have an opportunity to maximize their talents and skills, then make a commitment to put the proper fuel in their bodies and get them involved in physical activities.

Remember, you are building their habits—habits that will carry them for the rest of their lifetime. You're the role model, and so maybe this is the time for you to make some adjustments on what you have around the house, or just monitor their intake and make certain they're getting proper nutrition. Give them the chance to be their best. Great job! Take it to The Next Level!

CHAPTER 20

Discipline

As I've interviewed hundreds of parents, virtually all of them believe that discipline is a necessary part of being a successful parent. How about you? What is your belief about discipline and raising kids? My experience tells me that you believe the same: that discipline is a necessary part of raising successful kids.

The question is, what's your definition of discipline? Here's what I've seen as a parent. There's an inverse relationship between the parent's childhood and what the parent is practicing with the kids today. If there was extreme discipline in the home when the parent was a child, today the parent won't want to make the child feel bad, or won't want to be perceived as a "mean" parent or be as strict as the parent's parents were.

Let me be very clear here. The past does not equal the future, and that's a self-esteem issue. Let's talk about the big picture.

Suppose you have a 16-year-old boy in tenth grade—say, named Johnny—and Johnny's going out with some friends on Friday night after the football game. As he's walking out the door, you let him know that you want him home by midnight (which I think is pretty liberal). He acknowledges your request and he walks out the door. Fast forward—Johnny comes home at 1:00 A.M., and because you don't want to make him feel bad or because you were punished when you were a kid, you just let him slide, don't say anything, and don't discipline him. What time is he going to be coming home next Friday night? That's right, 2:00 A.M. or whenever he feels like it, because you set the tone. You made it okay for him not to recognize your request.

Tammy and I talk about this all the time, whether it's something as simple as this situation or whether it's bailing them out with the money issue. The parents aren't doing the kids any favors. They *think* they are, because they're coming to their rescue or being their friend. But the fact of the matter is that they're laying down a foundation of failure. Lack of discipline equals a lack of success.

The example of Johnny breaking a curfew is a no-brainer. But what's the difference between that situation and telling your eight-year-old to clean his room or brush her teeth and they don't? There's no difference. Any time parents allow their child to slip, they are setting the child up for failure.

Let's talk about the psychology of discipline. I believe it is extremely important to communicate with your kids starting a very, very young age. My daughter is eight and she's very clear about what she is to do or not do, what will happen if she fails, and why. Here's what I mean. You owe it to your children to give them the best shot at success, and working with very successful people as I do, I see a direct relationship between self-discipline and success as an adult. So the strategy we use in our home is based on three things: *rules*, *consequences*, and *reasons*.

RULES

So first things first. What are the rules in your home? What are your rules for respect? What are your rules at the dinner table? What are your rules for keeping their rooms tidy? What are your rules for developing a work ethic?

Let me give you an example. How many kids have you heard talking back to their parents? I mean, it's amazing. It really blows me away. In our house it's inappropriate to talk back to Tammy or myself. It just doesn't work. If I say to my son, "please pick up the living room before you brush your teeth," the only acceptable response is, "Yes, Daddy." That's it. Not, "I'm busy," or, "I don't feel like it," or, "Why don't you help me?" "Yes, Daddy," is *the* answer. It's very simple: There must be rules and standards. You must implement them now, or you're in trouble later.

Here's the philosophy that'll hold true with your kids. *If you don't have respect and discipline up front, you won't have it at the end.* You can take that to the bank. If you allow your six-year-old to challenge you now, you're setting the table for future challenges.

So again, what are your rules? There's no right or no wrong here, because we all have different views, philosophies, and values, yet you must establish your rules, whatever they are. That's Step 1.

CONSEQUENCES

When rules are broken, there must be negative consequences. Now, here's where it gets a little tricky, and there's a lot of room for error.

First and foremost, I'm not suggesting you discipline your child in this or that specific way rather than another. That's up to you. That depends on what you believe. What's important is that *you actually do it.* Empty threats and promises are as dangerous as no rules. This is where you as a parent must understand why you're enforcing your rules. Remember, it's not for you; it's for your children.

One of the biggest, most valuable gifts you can give your children is the gift of discipline and the concept of rules. Presents, toys, cars, games, they're all meaningless. They're all just temporary gifts—until the kids want what's next. Discipline and respect will take them places where no other gift will. They will last a lifetime.

And, by the way, discipline and respect have nothing to do with money. You're not able to buy discipline. Discipline comes with parents who have enough self-confidence and self-esteem that they can see the big picture versus the short-term reward.

Now, in order to create patterns there must also be positive consequences as well as negative. When your child follows the rules, there needs to be acknowledgment or praise. I don't mean buying something for good behavior. A simple, verbal message will do wonders. So, Step 2 is that there must be consequences, depending on whether the child follows the rules or does not follow them.

REASONS

This step is where we've taken it to the next level so that our kids understand the big picture. We have very clear conversations with our kids. When we have a challenge, so to speak, and I discipline my kids, they are very clear as to why. I have told them that it's my job to make sure they're very successful and I have to do whatever it takes to build the foundation of success.

I also tell them that Jesus is watching me and it's my job to make them successful. Now, regarding Jesus, that's my belief. Yet, whatever your religion or none, I think you all know where we're going with that. Kids must understand the why for discipline. Actually, I have clients whom I coach who like that strategy for themselves. They say it helps keep their psychology when they're disciplining their children.

In addition, we take every opportunity to show our kids what a lack of discipline leads to. When we see a homeless person on the street or someone begging for money, I explain to my kids that that person begging for money didn't have parents who demanded that he be his best. Now, of course, I'm sensitive to people and their circumstances, so I'm not poking fun in any way, and I know that anything can happen to anyone. Yet I use those real-life examples to give our kids a visual example of what life could be like without a Mommy and Daddy to discipline them. It's my job.

So the bottom line is this: You were blessed with one or more children who deserve the best chance to succeed. Success is not defined by what they wear, their toys, or what they get to do. Their success is defined by their ability to make decisions on their own and hold themselves accountable. The only way that kind of muscle is built is by parents who get the big picture and have the self-confidence and self-esteem to demand the best from their children.

Now, here's a potential challenge. It is absolutely imperative for Mom and Dad to be on the same page here. Even if you are divorced, you still must be on the same page to make this work. It does your children no good to have a stern father and a pushover mother, or vice versa. Consistency is the key.

Kids love discipline. They do! I believe a child with no discipline feels as though her parents really don't care about her, which leads her to find what she thinks is love and connection in other places.

So here's your Action Plan for this chapter:

Right now rate you and your partner's discipline with your kids, on a scale of 0 to 10. Where is it? 5? 6? 10? Or 2? Then ask yourself the follow-up question: Is it where it needs to be?

If not, make a decision today to raise the bar on the discipline in your house and remember the three steps to creating discipline:

1. Define your rules.
2. Make sure there are consequences for not following them and praise for following them.
3. Let your kids know why you're holding them to higher standards: because you love them and you want them to have the best chance to succeed. It's your job.

Great job! Let's take it to The Next Level!

CHAPTER 21

Belief, the Foundation of Success

Throughout this book I've talked about beliefs. They're the foundation of our success or our failure. You know that beliefs drive your behavior. What you believe determines what you do. For now, I'll give you a very abbreviated recap. A belief is a sense of certainty. It's how certain you are about something.

I'll give you an example. On a scale of zero to ten, ten being absolutely certain and zero not being certain at all, how certain are you that the sun's going to set tonight? Obviously, a ten.

In order to raise champions you must:

1. Believe in yourself.
2. Believe in your children.

BELIEVING IN YOURSELF

Here's what I mean. If you believe you're not a very good parent or that you don't have the resources to be a great parent, guess what? You're right. Beliefs drive your behavior. You won't be able to get yourself to do things you don't believe are possible.

So, first things first. No matter who you are or where you're from, how much money you make or what's going on in your life, you have the ability to be a great parent. To help you make the shift to being that great parent, I teach what I call the "as if" strategy. Acting *as if* you are who you really want to be.

Think about it. If you really were a great parent right now, the kind of parent whom other parents admire, the kind of parent whom people respect, the kind of parent who's shown on the cover of *Parents* Magazine—if that were you right now, how would you treat your children today? How patient would you be? How much time would you spend with them? How much love would you show them? What would you do differently today?

I used this strategy early in my children's lives to develop me into the father that I am today. No one knows all the answers, so when I would be confronted with a situation where I might have been frustrated or there was a behavior that required some type of discipline, I would ask myself, "If you were an outstanding parent, how would you handle the situation?" And then, of course, I took action. After a while of acting as if, I started to believe that I was an outstanding father. Now, I know I am an outstanding father.

Remember, beliefs drive your behavior. So if you believe you're a great parent, then you will do what a great parent does. Give it a shot. It's fun, and it works!

BELIEVING IN YOUR CHILDREN

Secondly, you must believe in your children. I mean, how can you teach someone to have a high self-esteem when you don't have any esteem for that someone yourself?

None of us had a perfect childhood, and if we could, many of us would change how our childhoods were. I can understand that, yet my message is this: Get over it. I mean, it's time for you now to give your child the best. If your parents didn't believe in you, don't give your child the same feelings. Build your children up.

Remember, belief drives your behavior. So, if you believed that your child was special, talented, and able to do anything he or she wanted to do, how would you guide them? How understanding would you be? How positive would you be? How much love and encouragement would you give them? It's that simple: acting as if.

So here's your Action Plan:

Act today as if you are a great parent.

Act as if you were the parent that you really want to be, or act as if you were the best parent in the world. What would you do? How much love would you give? How much time would you spend with your children? How much patience would you have? And act as if your children were special—that your children could do anything. How much guidance would you give them? How much encouragement would you give them? How much positivity would you give them? Simply act as if. Give it a shot. Great job! Go take it to The Next Level!

PART

Relationships at the Next Level

CHAPTER 22

Making Your Relationship Successful

I'm excited about this section because having a successful relationship is such an important part of our fulfillment as people, and at the same time, relationships are a challenge for many people. Just look at the numbers. Over 50 percent of marriages end in divorce, and that speaks loudly about the complexity of a relationship. But that's only the reported numbers. What do you think the percentage is of people who are in relationships or stay married, but aren't happy?

These chapters are not just for people who are married. This is for anyone involved in a relationship who has the desire to make it work. I want to acknowledge all of you for really stepping up and taking a look at your relationship. If your relationship's great, hey, that's fantastic; how can you make it better? And if it's not, well, let's pick up some tools that work.

Now, let me be very clear: Dan Lier, the 10 Minute Coach, is not proclaiming to be an expert in the field of relationships. We will leave that for the experts. I chose to share this information because I meet so many people who are having challenges in their relationships yet really want to make them successful. In addition, my wife, Tammy, and I have been together for over a decade and have been confronted with challenges, obstacles, and setbacks, yet we've found ways to keep the connection, attraction, and respect that many relationships lose over time. Tammy and I went through a six-year period during which we moved over 30 times because of the work I was doing. We had two children during that time, and I can honestly say that not many other people I know could have, or would have, kept it all together for those years.

With that in mind, we have created some strategies that work for us and have helped numerous others as well. Like many other people, we are both busy pursuing and building our businesses while raising children; thus, we balance business, family, and relationship issues on a daily basis.

This section is designed for both men and women. As a man, I am very sensitive to "relationship" advice from books, CDs, and so forth, because I've never found something that I could relate to. So, when I speak with men, they seem to "get" what I am sharing because for the first time they've heard it from a guy they can relate with. After an event I performed, I had a guy tell me, "Hey, Dan, listen. I'm a guy just like you. I watch Monday Night Football. Matter of fact, I watch Sunday football. I like to work out, have a good time. I'm committed to my family, but I'm a man's man, and this is the first time I've heard it from a guy I can relate with." And I take pride in that.

My experience with men and women all over the country is that many people are looking for ways to throw a wrench in other people's relationships, find out what the faults are in other relationships, to make themselves feel better. It's pathetic, yet true. I really hope these chapters help you understand that, as with anything else in life, it's up to *you*.

As adults we want to have successful relationships, we want to be happy, we want to be in love, and so forth. Yet, like anything else, it takes commitment. And here I don't mean commitment in the sense of making a promise to the other person. I mean commitment to working on yourself, working on your weak points, in order to improve as a person and be someone who would attract a happy relationship.

So this is the real deal. As you know, I'm a believer in you get out of life what you put in. You have the ability to make a decision and be your best in the relationship—the best listener you can be; the best friend you can be; the sexiest partner you can be. It's up to you.

With that in mind, read at least one chapter per day for at least two weeks, and you'll be on your way to a successful relationship. Let's take it to The Next Level!

CHAPTER 23

Respect

This is a great topic for people. I believe that respect is the foundation of any successful relationship. To be in a successful intimate relationship, you must have respect in two areas: respect for your partner and respect for yourself.

Now, when you think about respect, what does that mean to you? When you respect someone, you hold that person in a place of honor. The person has earned your respect as a result of how the person lives and acts or what the person has accomplished.

THE RESPECT RULE

In a relationship, it's imperative that you hold your partner in the highest of honor around other people. Now here's what I mean. Countless times I've been out with some guy, whether it's business or social, and he starts bagging on his wife or his girlfriend. I've heard blatant disrespect, such as telling how messy she is or how she doesn't want sex any more, and subtle disrespect, such as saying she's just always late. Now of course I don't know this for sure, but I'm confident the same thing happens when a group of women get together.

Now, I'm not saying that small talk and a little joking here and there is all bad. What is damaging to the relationship is talking in a derogatory fashion and putting your partner down blatantly in front of others. This is incredibly damaging and two-faced in the relationship.

The bottom line is that if you're putting your spouse down in front of others, the challenge is much deeper than just a little joke. When you air your dirty laundry in the form of casual chitchat with someone else, particularly another person of the same sex as your partner, you are sending a message of infidelity. It's okay to confide in a really great friend, but to dog your mate on a regular basis is absolutely unacceptable.

Tammy and I have a strategy we use in our relationship to prevent anything close to this happening, and we call it the *respect rule*. Here's what it means. It means that it's never OK— and I mean *never*—to talk in a negative manner about one another in front of others. It's that simple. It's black and white. It's a line. And I know this sounds simple. Yet in our ten-plus years together, I have always held Tammy in the highest respect around other people. It just doesn't make sense to talk about your partner in a derogatory manner in front of anyone else. Save any complaints for your "personal and private" times. The respect rule keeps things tight. Tammy and I have certainty that we're never disrespecting each other in the presence of others.

A few years back, a friend of ours named Carol was having a conversation with two women whom she considered pretty good friends. They brought something to her attention. One woman asked, "Carol, do you and Greg ever have problems?" And the other woman chimed in, "Yeah, you never come to us with complaints or issues in your relationship." At first, Carol laughed and said, "Oh, my goodness, come on." Then she said, "Hey, listen. My relationship is not perfect, by any means. So first of all, let's get something real clear here. I respect my relationship enough that I address these issues on a regular basis with Greg, not open my mouth every month with you ladies, who are just aching to hear about my issues."

Carol said she elaborated more, and by the end of her conversation with these women they totally understood, because they realized that putting their partners down on a consistent basis is incredibly counterproductive in manifesting a powerful relationship.

Let's be honest. When you're dogging your mate, who really looks like the fool? If I talk in a derogatory manner about

Tammy in front of others, this really sends a message about my lack of confidence, and it's a direct reflection on me. It's funny, because when I hear other men dogging their partners in front of a group of men, I think to myself, "Gee, if she's so bad, what are you doing with her?"

It's interesting that you can apply the same simple strategy, the Respect Rule, in business. In order to build relationships and grow your reputation and your business, you must not talk about other business contacts in a derogatory fashion in front of others with whom you are doing business.

When you dog your partner in front of others, pretty soon all of your friends know about your partner's shortcomings, and they label your partner to yet others. All of a sudden, other people are referring to your partner as "airhead," "the jerk," or something even more colorful. How would you like to be referred to as "deadbeat dad" or "lazy"? Even if such labels are true, keep it "in the family." When you disrespect your partner in front of others, you are essentially giving others the permission to show disrespect as well. It just doesn't work for a long-term partnership.

THE PRIVACY FACTOR

In addition to the respect rule, we practice something I refer to as the *privacy factor*. When you respect somebody, you treat this person as a treasure. You then guard the relationship's value by maintaining its privacy.

When you air your dirty laundry with other friends, give others "the inside scoop," and share your business with everyone else—you actually make the issue bigger than what it really is. When the issue comes out in the open and becomes the topic of other people's conversation, it becomes more real to you as well.

Think about that. The issue isn't really that big in the first place. Yet if you choose to go and air it out, share it with eight friends, guess what? They remind you every time they see you. "Oh, how's the jerk?" Then you've opened up the floodgates. You've given people a license to talk about your partner as well.

This is *not good* for a long-term relationship. Others then bring your focus back, over and over, on the things that have bothered you about your partner, and, as a human being, whatever you focus on, you get. Whatever you focus on gets bigger to you. So if you start focusing on talking about your wife's issues or your husband's issues, then more and more people get to talking about it with you, and they keep you focused on your complaint, which gets bigger and bigger and bigger until it's a problem.

So here's your Action Plan for today.

If you've got something that's not positive to say about your partner in front of others, whether they're acquaintances or best friends, just shut up and hold it in. If you don't have something great to say, then just don't say it.

Hold your partner in the highest of honor. Implement the respect rule. It's really a simple strategy, yet it works for myself and other successful people. Give it a shot. Great job! Take it to The Next Level!

CHAPTER 24

Communication

Now hey, this is an original topic, huh? I bet you would have never thought of this one! Well, communication plays a major role in the success of my relationship and, quite frankly, the demise of many others' relationships.

Tammy and I probably overcommunicate, if there is such a thing. It enables us to know how we both feel, rather than wondering what's going on.

I know this is a bit difficult for me, because my natural tendency as a man is to keep things in, just because I feel I am (or should be) able to handle it, or maybe that whatever I'm feeling just isn't that important. That's fine in theory, yet here's what used to happen: I would let things build up, and then one day I'd just be overly sarcastic or snide or rude because of the resentment I had built up. Tammy wouldn't know where this was coming from, so she probably thought I was being some kind of jerk or something. That cycle isn't good for the longevity of any relationship.

THREE WAYS NOT TO COMMUNICATE

In my years of coaching people about successful relationships, whether business or personal, I have seen that, a majority of the time, the bottom-line issue was, and still is, a breakdown or gap in the communication between oneself and the other person.

A good friend of mine who is a relationship coach believes there are three ingredients that persist in unhealthy communication:

1. *Judging one another.* This means jumping to conclusions based on a perception and creating a false reality of what is going on.
2. *Misinterpretation.* This leaves no room for understanding what is really going on and inclines you to create a false story quickly.
3. *Selective listening.* This is basically hearing what you want to hear. Men get a bad rap for that one . . . and quite frankly, over the years, I have been guilty of selective listening.

So there you have it: the perfect ingredients to a relationship headed for doom. Yikes, how do you like this chapter so far?

THE RED ZONE

I want to be totally up front. As a man, I still do hold many things in, because in any relationship there are many things that could bother someone. Yet I do make sure I communicate on issues or behaviors that are in the red zone—what I call the divorce zone.

This is a terminology I came up with because, like many men, I'm a football fan, and I've found that when I'm talking with other men about things like relationships, to make any sense, I need to put it in terms we are all familiar with, and it's easy to remember. For those of you who aren't football fans, the red zone on the football field is the part between the 20-yard line and the goal line. It's the scoring zone. So when a team has the ball inside their red zone, they push extra hard because they need to put some points on the board—and the defense has to push extra hard to keep them from doing it.

With that in mind, when something bothers me enough that if it were to continue, it could lead to divorce, I call it the divorce zone, or DZ.

So here's how it works for me. When something is bothering me, whether it's something that Tammy said or something she did (or didn't do), before I respond I'll ask myself: "Is this something that, if she continued to do and never changed, would cause me to want a divorce?" Now, if the answer is yes, then it's in the DZ, and I always communicate.

And I ask this question because sometimes in our relationship things bother me, yet when I take a second to really look at what the issue is, I find that sometimes I'm just being oversensitive or short or impatient, so I deal with it myself. I mean, let's face it. When you're in a relationship, there are two people living their lives together with different wants, needs, backgrounds, and idiosyncrasies, and there are just going to be upsets and disagreements. So that's part of the deal, and it's important for you to know what the real potential issues are.

I'll give you a simple example. Tammy comes home, she's busy. She's a career woman, she's picking up kids, rushing here, rushing there. She's got a lot of things going. We've got an island in the middle of our kitchen, and when she comes home, she drops off her purse, the groceries, the kids' homework, lunches, all kinds of stuff on the island. I like to keep the island clean, so it kind of bothers me. We've talked about it, and sometimes she still leaves stuff on the island, because she's on fire, she's on the run, faster than the proverbial speeding bullet. So I walk in, and the island is cluttered, and I'll say to myself, "The island is messy." If for some reason it's really bothering me, I'll ask myself the question: "If she were to continue leaving stuff there, would that be a big thing for me? I mean, she's loving, she's kind, she's amazing, she's a great mother, she's fun, she's passionate. So if the island's dirty, is it that big a deal for me?" And the answer is no. So that's how I work. It's not brain surgery, yet it keeps me focused on what's really important.

MORE EFFECTIVE COMMUNICATION STRATEGIES

This is the very reason why learning the most effective strategies for your relationship is paramount. If you want to give your relationship the best chance for survival, you must commit to effective communication strategies.

Here are a few others you may find helpful:

1. You must first communicate with yourself effectively on the following items:

   a. Why are you in this relationship?
   b. What feelings must you feel on a consistent basis in order to have a thriving relationship?
   c. How can you take responsibility today for actively pursuing your relationship?

2. You must get honest, quick, with your partner.

Oftentimes, people don't want to hurt each other. "Oh, I don't want to hurt his or her feelings. I don't want to say that." Listen, you might think you're doing your partner a favor by not communicating something negative. You're not. You're inhibiting one another; you're keeping each other from growing in the relationship. You're holding each other back. You're holding back the truth. I learned a long time ago that telling the truth later gets harder. Think about that. Think back at all those times that you waited to be totally honest.

TELLING THE TRUTH FIRST

Tammy and I have something we call "Who Can Tell the Truth First?" When you tell the truth first, everything's out on the table, and the communication really takes off.

Think of a time when you waited for days or weeks or even years until you were finally able to tell your partner the truth about some situation or feelings. It doesn't matter what the situation was; it could be something that happened to you way back when, or it could be something current in your relationship that you haven't addressed. You spared your own feelings and your desires. You chose not to share, thinking that you were protecting the relationship. Were you really helping or hurting yourself? I would guarantee that while you were preventing yourself from being totally honest, you experienced higher levels of stress in your life.

So, the bottom line is to get to the bottom line as quickly as possible.

Now, I have a message especially for the guys here. We've already talked about the Divorce Zone, and now here's some bonus information at no extra charge.

One of the challenges I've had is that when I did choose to communicate with Tammy about how I felt, I used to do it in an accusatory fashion—basically, tell her what she did wrong (meaning what I didn't like). Right away, that would put anyone on the defensive, and the conversation didn't go as smoothly as I planned.

So, guys, here's the key, and I know it's a stretch. It's something different, yet it's how women communicate. If something's bothering you, don't accuse her and tell her what she did wrong. Tell her how *you* feel. Here, repeat after me:

> Honey, I'd like to share something with you. This is how I feel about this.

Wow, that's even difficult for me to write! (I'm just being facetious.) Yet this is an area that I've really had to commit to working on in order for my relationship to grow.

Women like to talk about feelings because they're more used to "feeling" than we are. So talk about it in their language. Tell them how you feel, how you're bothered by it, how you might be frustrated by it, how you feel a certain way because of it. You'll get open ears, and it will really open up the communication process. Women tell me that they like it when men actually share their feelings. When a man shares something that's in his heart, the women are actually going to listen. No offense, guys. Just keeping it real.

Of course, this is not easy, yet it works. Tammy and I have been together for over ten years, two kids, busy, in love, traveling, working through life's opportunities and challenges, and you know what? It takes extra effort to really make it work.

So here's your Action Plan for this chapter.

Make a commitment to communicate. Overcommunicate, even. Tell the person how you feel, what's going on, what you're thinking, how you're feeling. And if something's both-ering you that's big enough to be in the divorce zone, tell the person about it. Don't hold it in. Tell the truth first.

So that's your plan. Overcommunicate. Talk about it. Be open-minded. Tell him or her how you feel. Great job! Take it to The Next Level!

CHAPTER 25

Self-Esteem

As I have coached people over the years, in business and in life, I've found that self-esteem is paramount to a healthy relationship. And it's not just the man having self-esteem or the woman having high self-esteem. The key is *both* people in the relationship having a healthy self-esteem.

Now, why is that important? I know when Tammy and I met, what attracted me to her was that she didn't need me, which, quite frankly, was a different experience for me. And let me be real clear. I'm not Mr. Tom Cruise or anything. It's simply that many women I met over the years seemed to be looking for a man—or worse, looking for someone to save them.

When I met Tammy, I wasn't looking for a relationship. I was looking to better myself and climb the ladder of success, and she wasn't looking for a man, so there was an instant respect we had for each other. She had goals. She had things she wanted to achieve in her life, and I was attracted to that. As a result, I treated her differently than I would have treated Ms. Last Week or Ms. Last Night, so to speak, because Tammy was on her own path. I knew that if I wanted our paths to cross even a little, I needed to treat her with respect and alter my behaviors to match a woman who demanded that respect.

SELF-ESTEEM THROUGH ACHIEVING GOALS

I want to be very clear here: I am not proclaiming Dan Lier, the 10 Minute Coach, as some type of relationship expert. I'm simply sharing some things that work for us. I like to keep things real, keep them in perspective, and I understand that many people have challenges in their relationships. So, if I can help just a little, I'll offer a few strategies that have worked for us.

When it gets right down to it, self-esteem is how you feel about yourself. It's that simple. And you develop that feeling of self-esteem or self-worth by what you have accomplished in your own mind, meaning, by having moved your life in a positive direction—by achieving goals.

I think all people have the desire to be their best, which is why I'm so committed to see people achieve. When I talk about goals, I don't mean they have to be huge. I mean, huge is only in the eyes of the beholder. Goals can be earth-shattering, or they may be very simple, such as to eat three servings of fruit each day for the next week. That's a goal.

When you reach a goal, what happens is that it sends a message of self-worth to your unconscious mind, which makes you feel better about yourself. That is how self-esteem develops.

In our relationship, Tammy and I get together at least once every 90 days and talk about our personal and our business goals. I realize that strategy is not for everyone. Yet we've committed to that to keep us connected. Unconsciously, it helps us be accountable to one another, knowing the other person knows what we're looking to achieve.

PURPOSE AND PURPOSELESSNESS

One of my good friends was married to a beautiful woman; let's call these people "Jim" and "Theresa." Theresa had been previously married and so had Jim. They met, fell in love, and they were married. When Tammy and I met them, we went to dinner, had conversations, and really got to know each other. Tammy and I both perform coaching, and so we hear conversations a bit differently than other people do. We hear language patterns and how the people feel about themselves. We pick up behaviors and tendencies. We were talking about life, about careers, kids, sports, fitness, sex, the whole gamut, if you will. We would ask questions like "So, what's your focus for this year?" or "What are you most proud of?" or "What are your top three goals this year?" The response we kept getting from Theresa was, "Well, Jim said I should do this." "Well, Jim said I should do that." "And Jim said" . . . "and Jim said"—and Tammy and I were looking at each other, thinking, "what about *her*?"

So I finally asked her, "Theresa, what about *you*? What do *you* want to do?" And it was amazing. She paused, she looked at Jim, and she said, "Well, Jim and I have to talk about that." Wow! Now, I'm all for partnerships—Tammy and I are partners—but that's a little ridiculous. Quite frankly, Theresa didn't have a life. And I don't mean to be cruel, but she just didn't have anything she was striving for, for her own reasons.

A successful person once told me, "You're either living a life purposefully or purposelessly." To create a successful, respectful relationship, you must be just a tad self-reliant. I mean, make some decisions. Set some goals. Build your self-esteem.

Understand that your purpose drives your behavior. If, as you go through each day, you find yourself making strides and hitting small achievements and feeling great, your self-esteem eventually will rise to a level where you are feeling strong and confident. It's just every day, making those incremental steps and those changes in your life, a result you'll manifest over time.

Your Self-Esteem and Your Partner

Now, one thing that makes your self-esteem powerful in your relationship is that if you feel special already, you can make that someone in your life feel special as well. It's such an easier conversation than you being always dissatisfied with the other and ridiculing or criticizing because you are dissatisfied with yourself.

It's that simple. Goals can be very simple in any area of your life. For example:

- ❏ "I'm going to make certain that my youngest can read complete sentences by Christmas." That's a simple goal.
- ❏ "I'm going to be the best mother I can possibly be this week, and here's how I'm going to do it."
- ❏ "I'm going to make my wife feel like a princess this week."
- ❏ "I'm going to bring her flowers at least twice a month."
- ❏ "I'm going to advance my career and get in better shape."

It's up to you!

By setting your goal to be a better parent, a better daughter, a better brother, better sister, better spouse, you're also being an example. And if you knew that you were the example for someone else, you'd set a lead that they would want to follow.

So that's important in a relationship. It's not just one having self-esteem or just the other. You both have to have self-esteem. Tammy and I are working on our own goals personally, which makes us feel better about each other.

So here's your Action Plan:

Think about some things you want to accomplish—maybe some things you haven't been doing that you really want to do—and put a game plan together. Take some action today that you haven't taken yesterday or you didn't do the day before or the week before. Maybe it's going for a walk. Maybe it's eating three servings of fruit today. Maybe it's telling your spouse how much you love him or her. Whatever it is, do something different. Raise the bar for yourself.

Go out and take some action. Develop your self-esteem. Great job! Take it to The Next Level!

CHAPTER 26

Intimacy

If you read any books or watch any talk shows, I'd say we all agree that men and women are wired differently in respect to intimacy. Now, neither is right or wrong; we're just a little different.

As a matter of fact, studies show that most of all divorces are attributed to the lack of intimacy or the lack of money. I'll share with you firsthand that when the intimacy is great, the money just doesn't seem to be as big an issue.

Now, let's understand something. I've consulted with both men and women. It's interesting because I'm hired as a success consultant, yet after the trust is built, both men and women open up the relationship subject, because it's such a major part of all of our lives.

THE INTIMACY WOMEN WANT

According to numerous experts—and I call them experts because when it comes to relationships, women are the experts—women typically look for emotional intimacy; that is, often times, women want to be talked to, to be asked questions about their life and about how they feel. Women long for conversation, and it fulfills them as whole persons. They love to be asked questions. They love to be asked how their day was. And they love for their man (partner, spouse, mate) to say to them, "Hey, tell me a little bit about your life."

Men, on the other hand, often want to cut to the chase. Now I know I'm generalizing. Yet I talk to men every day, and this is more true than not. Now, often those two issues collide for people in relationships, and it pertains to intimacy. So let's discuss this a little further.

And again, Tammy and I are sharing with you strategies that we've found to work. Tammy and I have been together for ten years. It's been a great time. We have two beautiful children. We enjoy a loyal, intimate relationship.

The Intimacy Men Want

Tammy's my second wife. Now, my first relationship was a little bit different. Yeah, I was younger, immature, wasn't so secure about myself, and, quite frankly, I wasn't loyal. I mean, I wanted to be. I intended to be. Yet it just didn't happen. Yeah, ultimately, it was my decision. It was my responsibility that I went somewhere else for that intimacy. However, I'll let you know that I wasn't getting it at home. And not to say that it was right what I did, but we're going to talk about what works.

When I look at the successful relationships that I've been exposed to, the woman has an "understanding" and appreciation of the man's needs. I'm not being sexist here, nor am I suggesting that's it's all about the man. Yet we've identified the woman's need for conversation, and the men typically are driven by a different need. We all know this. If this is a news-flash to you, well then—it's time to wake up!

Based on the clients I've coached and the research that I've done with both men and women, there's a lot of "room for error" when you've mastered the art of intimacy. When you are able to do that, you will realize that you'll get exactly what you want in the relationship. Because what it really comes down to is your confidence and your belief about what intimacy is.

Tammy had a client, a woman who was about 110 pounds overweight, yet she had a belief about herself as it pertained to her intimacy. She believed she was the best lover on earth! Her man loved her, and she spoke openly about the fact that she was a great lover. She would say how much she loved to hug him, caress him, and make him feel great as if "he was the man!"

So, understand, ladies—you don't have to look like a swimsuit model. You just have to have the mindset. How do you set that mindset up? Ask yourself one question. If I absolutely knew that through my attitude and my attitude alone, I would make this person, my partner, feel like the best, sexiest person on earth, how would that next dictate my move, and how would I operate on an intimate level?

INTIMACY IN A BUSY WORLD

Let's face it; we live in a busy society. People are working hard to support their families and build their future, and sometimes "life can get in the way." I'll give you a couple of examples about what could be happening out there. Americans across the country work hard, and in most cases these days, both the man and the woman are working. The man comes home after a long day, and the woman comes home after a long day, and maybe the woman's feeling affectionate, or she wants to talk or she wants to have some intimacy, and the guy's feeling, "I'm just tired. I've been working all day. I just feel sweaty and dirty." And there's some flirting going on, but he's not buying in.

Or, how about this one? The wife's been home all day with the two kids and the man comes home after a long day, getting it done, meeting goals. He's feeling good and she's tired—dead tired. I know I've had clients who talk about this one. He wants intimacy, and she's just not in the mood.

For the most part, both people are working in the relationship; they have a busy schedule. Especially when they have children, there's a lot going on. You have business meetings. You have family coming in. You have family leaving. A lot of stuff comes up.

So you have to make intimacy a priority in your life. Let's be really clear. Intimacy is extremely important in the relationship to build it to the next level and to keep that fire burning consistently and keep it thriving. Why is that? The bottom line is that we are both emotional creatures and physical creatures. We are beings who like to have certain feelings met and fulfilled.

CREATING OPPORTUNITIES

This sounds funny as we are talking about intimacy in relationships, yet I've found that this philosophy is appropriate. You've probably heard the Latin motto *carpe diem*: Seize the moment, baby! Make it happen. Tammy and I live by that strategy.

We're busy. I mean, Tammy and I are both out pursuing things, careers, building our business. We have kids, soccer, tennis . . . the list goes on.

I mean, come on! If you think that we're coming home and putting the lights down, flicking on some Barry White, and getting out the oils, that's just not happening. We'd like it to happen; it just doesn't happen as frequently as we'd like.

So we seize the moment. We have to take advantage of any opportunity we can, and that all starts with the attitude for intimacy. Having an open mind about what it means, seizing the moment, and really, just being playful with it. Women have shared with me that this is a mindset. Some women think they need to have the mood be just right, or have the setting be just perfect, or have their man say the perfect phrase. Come on, ladies. Women (and men) who have mastered the art of intimacy have a confidence and a powerful perspective on what intimacy is that can overcome surprising obstacles.

And remember—keep this in mind—that most of the time women and men pretty much want the same things; they just have different ways of sharing what they want.

So here are your Action Plans for this chapter.

Men, ask some more questions about her and listen to what she has to say. I know it's a big stretch for you, yet if you're not getting what you want, there's a reason for that. Women have shared with me that when they don't feel connected with their man, they don't feel "in the mood." In addition, do something different. Say some nice words. Be romantic. Light some candles. Do something different from what you did yesterday. What would you do if you were in the first week of the relationship? Take some action in regard to intimacy.

Ladies, spice it up. That's all I've gotta say. Make something happen that you haven't been doing in the relationship, as it pertains to intimacy. Make a new choice. Whisper in his ear. Grab his shoulder. Grab his hand. Massage his shoulders. Pick up a new outfit, whatever—do something that you haven't been doing that you know you should do and make it happen.

Great job today! Go take it to The Next Level!

CHAPTER 27

Expectations

What Tammy and I have found is that many people don't set the expectations when they get into their relationship. They start dating and the sparks start flying; things are exciting. And they move to the next level, where they get serious—they fall in love. Then they decide they want to get married and spend the rest of their lives together. And then things change.

Yeah, I know it's cliché, yet it's true. Things change. The other person's behavior, attitude, how the person treats you, how you treat the person, the intimacy, the physical appearance. Many things can happen. So here's what's worked for Tammy and me in regard to expectations. We have laid out the expectations in our marriage in three specific areas: loyalty, attitude, and physical appearance.

It's a simple concept. You just have to be committed to play at a high level. When talking about a successful relationship, playing at the highest level is the only level that works.

LOYALTY

First of all, let's talk about our loyalty. I mean, it's on the table with Tammy and me. It's no secret; it's no mystery. I mean, literally, I can decide to hook up with any other woman any time I want, but there are a few consequences: Tammy's gone, my kids are gone, and half of what we've worked for is gone. It's that simple. And the same goes for her. If Tammy chooses to be unfaithful, which is a choice, I'm out, no questions about it, and she knows it. Those are the standards we set up. That's the expectation, and it works for us.

Once you set those standards up, it gets really easy. I mean, let's face it. There are temptations everywhere, okay? If you're looking for some action, I guarantee you can find it. Being in the business that we are in, we have different things that come up and different people whom we meet in our lives. This is not unique by any means. If you are in a relationship, you are faced with the same issues—or, should I say, *choices.* You're at work, meeting new people, face to face or on the phone. Business meetings, travel, company parties, you name it. It's there for you if you want it.

The bottom line is, if you invite opportunity into you life and if you leave that door open for someone, and you're not clear about the expectations for your relationship and your loyalty in that relationship, someone's going to come in and crack that door open a little farther. The door gets cracked, the foot slips in the door, and there you go.

So here's a strategy that works. We call it the "phone call strategy." Here's how it works. If a situation ever arises in which you are about to make a choice to be unfaithful to your spouse, you must pick up the phone and let your spouse know what you are about to do. Tammy and I use this strategy in our relationship, and guess how many calls we've made. That's right, *none.* Can you imagine that phone call? No way, baby, not me!

Now the reality is that this strategy goes only as far as someone's integrity, meaning that if someone is going to be unfaithful in the first place, chances are the person won't have the guts to dial the spouse on the phone and tell them what's happening. With that in mind, it really comes down to respect—the respect you have for your partner. If you respect your partner as a person in your life, then you owe that person the respect to tell the truth. So the phone call strategy works for us.

You see, that's a standard. Again, we're talking about playing at a high level, and this is what it's all about. It's easy to talk about playing at the highest level in business, yet what about the relationship? Expectation equals standards—a standard for living. What I've learned—not just coaching people, but in everyday society too—is that many people don't have those expectations, so guess what? Anything goes. Anything. "Oh, that just happened." "Oh, it was just a weird time in our relationship." Uh-uh. There's no "weird time." This is the deal. Let's communicate. Let's be clear with each other and give our relationship the best chance to succeed.

ATTITUDE

Tammy and I had expectations when we entered our relationship about what kind of attitude we would expect from one another.

When I met Tammy, one of things about her that was attractive to me was her attitude. She was so full of life. She's positive. One of the rules I had when I was single was that if I was going to get involved with someone, I was committed to be in a relationship with somebody who's going to bring something to the table. I mean, we're gonna play on the same surface; she's gonna enhance what I'm already doing. Tammy has a great attitude. So those are my expectations of her, and she's got the same ones of me, quite frankly.

We talk about this openly and we use the zero-to-ten scale just for fun. Ten is when you are feeling unstoppable, you're on fire, feeling great. Zero is a medical comatose. I mean, think about it. When people meet each other, they're usually at a level seven, eight, nine, or ten. They're at their best behavior. I mean, you're never going to attract somebody if you're down in the dumps. Oh, how are you doing today? "Well, things aren't so good. I feel bad. I'm depressed." Nobody wants to be around that.

Now, I understand, things come up. We have issues. We have challenges. Life throws us curve balls. That's okay. Handle it and get over it, but don't make it a habit. I mean, who wants to live with someone who brings them down?

PHYSICAL APPEARANCE

I've talked with enough women to know that this is a very touchy and challenging subject. Let's just put the cards on the table and talk about it, and then we'll find a way to make it work for us.

I had a very confident, successful woman share this analogy with me. She said, "Ladies, imagine if you bought this new home and you were just in love with it. It's your dream home. You fell in love with this home. It had all the bathrooms you wanted, the right floor plan, ceiling fans, lighting fixtures, a great backyard, I mean this house was made for you. So you purchase this home and then a week later, you move in and the home has changed. The interior paint is a different color. Two weeks later, it changes even more; the rooms are smaller. A year later, two years, three years, ten years, you don't even have the same home you started with."

The bottom line is, with no emotion attached to this story, you fell in love with a certain house, and that's the house you wanted. The same thing happens in relationships. I mean, I had a client, a very successful businessman, a nice guy. A great father, he was responsible; he took care of his business. He said, "Listen, I mean, I've gotta be honest with you. My wife—I did not buy this." I said, "What do you mean?" He answered, "No, no, no. I didn't sign the papers for what I have today." They'd been married for seven years. He continued, "She gained 35 pounds, okay, first of all. Second of all, she really has a poor attitude. Her attitude stinks." Now before we jump to conclusions, I've been around the block long enough to know that there are two sides to every story, yet this is conversation that I hear more than I'd like. My question for you, though, is, what did you buy into, day one, and what do you have now? And, who were *you* on day one and who are you now in that relationship? That's the real question.

This has nothing to do with your partner, if you really think about it. It has everything to do with *you*. And my intention is not to sound like it's so shallow, but the reality is, part of falling in love is attraction. You get attracted to somebody, and what attracted me to Tammy is, in part, the way she looks, obviously. Yeah, she's got a great attitude. Yeah, she has goals and dreams. And I love the way she looks.

That's not to say that if things were to change, I wouldn't love her as much. But, quite frankly, the attraction might not be there. We want the attraction to be always there as part of our relationship, so we hold each other to certain expectations in regard to our physical appearance. That's important to both of us. So those are our values. That's not to say that they work for you, but those work for us.

And just to be clear, this goes both ways. It's not just ladies, it's men. I mean, I meet so many guys on business who are carrying an extra 50 or 60 pounds yet complaining about their wives. That's absolutely not appropriate.

Here's a strategy that I use when I'm talking to guys and they start complaining about their wives. I ask them whether they've ever heard about the billboard strategy? They ask, "What is that?" I say, "Well, it's one of the strategies I use with my clients. When a guy starts complaining about his wife or his girlfriend or whoever, I say, if you're not comfortable with yourself being in a set of Calvin Kleins and being placed on one of those big billboards in your hometown in just your Calvin Kleins—if you're not comfortable with that, your own body, then you shouldn't be saying anything derogatory about your spouse or your girlfriend or anyone else, for that matter." It's just kind of a reality check and I think it goes both ways.

So here's your Action Plan for today.

Take a look at your expectations. What are your expectations for your loyalty, your intimacy, for your partner, and what about your attitude? Have you guys talked about your expectations as far as your attitude? And last but not least is your physical appearance. Maybe that's not important to you, but if it is, it's something you should talk about, because it comes up. I mean, ladies and gentlemen, it comes up. We're out there. Tammy and I are both coaching. We hear it from both men and women, so don't act like it's not there. Tell the truth first.

Expectations. Great job today. Take it to The Next Level!

CHAPTER 28

A Message to Women

Okay, ladies, this message is for you: just some thoughts from a man's perspective that may come in handy in regard to your relationship. Wherever you are in your relationship, whether you're just dating, divorced, married, separated, or getting back together, I believe that most situations can be mended if they're handled properly.

Now, from a man's perspective, he wants a woman by his side, a woman whom he can call his own who will stand by him through thick and thin. Knowing that, if you will, gives a man strength. So a foundational strategy for women in regard to communicating and showing a man love is her belief—belief in him as a man, his vision, his actions, his plans. So if you're in a relationship with a man, you must have believed in him at some point, to move forward in that relationship. This is important as we, as a couple, go through ups and downs in our lives and our relationships.

It wasn't long ago that I, along with many other people, made some poor decisions about investing during the dot-com craze, and we got hit hard. It was a Mike Tyson punch. It about knocked us out. But we built back up. Then I was enticed by a start-up company that made a nice executive offer, and I was excited about the potential future of this opportunity. Well, long story short, this company didn't make it, and we were hit hard again.

Tammy could have lost faith in me, or us, but she didn't. She believed in me. She stood by me, which gave me confidence and the drive to dig in even harder and make it happen. My point is that men need certainty. They need their partner to believe in them, to stand by them, to understand them through the good times and the challenging times.

Now, just to be clear, I'm conceptually speaking here. If your partner's making poor life choices or maybe he isn't motivated to be his best, that's something different. Stand by him, to some extent, and, as I've talked about, you must have standards and expectations. I mean, come on, dump the loser if he's not pulling his weight. Sorry, guys.

Secondly, remember, men are really easy. They have a few basic needs: food, water, sports, hobbies, and intimacy—whatever they like to do, and not necessarily in that order. His areas of interest may deviate from these, but all men have basic needs and interests. If you can focus on him getting his needs, he'll do anything for you. I'm an ex-college basketball player and an ex-college coach, so I still get enjoyment from playing basketball. So Tammy will ask me, "Hey, are you playing basketball today?" And she encourages me to do it, which satisfies my competitive and my athletic drive.

Men are simple. Food, water, sports, hobbies, and intimacy. We're really, really simple.

Now, what about intimacy? Let me give you some tips there. Plain and simple, men just want to feel desirable. I mean, listen, I'm with guys, and it doesn't matter where we are, when a woman says hi or if she smiles, most of the time the guys will respond to that. Men want to feel wanted. They want to feel desirable, which is really what they want.

The reality is, we want to be desired by our wife or our girlfriend. (And notice I said the word "or"—not wife "and" girlfriend. That's a whole other book.) When I'm getting ready to leave the house for a meeting or when I'm coming home from work, and Tammy says, "Hey, you look handsome" or "You look great" and then comes over and gives me a big hug or a kiss, it makes me feel great. I mean, that's what I need.

Now, honestly—and Tammy will tell you—I'm very secure and I don't really need that, yet I'll tell you that it's nice and I like it. And see, when Tammy's telling me this, if I'm out there and meet some love-starved vixen, so to speak, and she says, "Hey, Dan, you look great," and looks at me with those inviting eyes, it doesn't faze me. But if a man's not getting attention at home, he's gonna get it somewhere else, and guess where he's going to want to spend his time? It's that simple.

So, ladies, this is very simple. The Action Plan is this:

You gotta stand by your man. Believe in him—up and down—and stand by him. Give him certainty. He needs that. And also understand, he's got some certain needs he wants. He wants to enjoy himself, have certain hobbies, intimacy, those things. Give him those things and make him feel desirable and you're on your way to a great relationship.

It's really simple. Great job! Take it to The Next Level!

CHAPTER 29

A Message to Men

I'm going to let Tammy run with this one, because she coaches numerous women on their relationships, so she's obviously more qualified than I.

(Tammy:) This is my message, men, about the women in your life. There's one strategy, one thing specifically that comes to mind that you could master and be more effective at. Why do I know this? Because I've received numerous bits of feedback from women on their spouses, their mates, their boyfriends—you name it—and they have shared the same thing with me numerous times.

OK, you want to hear it? OK:

> "I wish he would ask more questions. Not only that,
> I wish he would actually be interested after the second
> question."

Now, this is real simple. It isn't rocket science. You guys are smart. You're making money. You're making things happen. You're creating results at work. You're supporting your family. You're doing so much at one time. I know you're demanding, and you know what? This is just another level that you can get to in your relationship that will cause your wife to feel great about herself, and you.

Now, keep in mind, women are most attached to the emotional intimacy. Now, I'm not saying every woman, yet by and large. So let me ask you a question. If you absolutely knew beyond a shadow of a doubt—I mean, absolutely knew—that by asking your partner better questions, you were going to cause her to think about you differently and look at you as the hot, sexy, desirable man in her life, that she just wanted to look at you and say, "Hey, baby"—you know what I'm saying—what would you do? And what if someone else was asking her questions? Who's that Romeo around the corner? So-and-so at the coffee shop who's gonna look at your spouse or your mate and ask her, "Hey, how you doing?" I mean, there's always room for that. So I'm telling you, it's a competitive world out there. Even though men are out there doing their thing, women are out there meeting people as well.

So my challenge for you—your Action Plan—is:

Ask effective questions. "How was your day?" Great. "Tell me about your day." Excellent. "Tell me more about your day." "Ah, what did that mean?"

I'm talking about challenging you to a level where you're just wanting your wife or your spouse or your mate to elaborate a little more than just those first one, two, three questions. We want to get you engaged in a conversation and get great at that, okay? That will develop a powerful relationship. Take it to The Next Level!

Epilogue

In closing, I want to thank you for allowing me to have an impact on your life. I truly believe that life is defined in moments. There are moments of decision that have an impact on your actions and ultimately affect your destiny.

The challenge is that we sometimes make decisions or take actions in an unresourceful state of mind, when our psychology is a bit weak and we act out of character, not truly being the person that we really are.

Even the most successful people need a little juice now and then, a pep talk, if you will. So, keep this book with you at all times, or invest in my CD series, *The 10 Minute Coach*, for your car when you need a little psychology shift so that you can be your best and maximize your opportunities.

If you'd like to book me for a corporate speaking event or enroll in our high-impact presentation training or performance coaching, call our corporate office at 888-254-1861, or email us at info@danlier.com. I'm Dan Lier, the 10 Minute Coach, wishing you the best in all your endeavors.

Call Dan Lier to Speak at your next corporate event!

When companies are looking to make their event an impactful and entertaining experience, they hire Dan Lier. With over 3,500 live presentations, Dan's track record speaks for itself. Dan's charismatic style and powerful delivery, makes any meeting a meeting to remember.

Keynotes, Kick-off Meetings, Company Events and Sales Events

"Dan's message enlightened our team on what's possible for themselves and our company. He has the unique ability to inspire in such a way that it relates our business and personal lives."
Alain Troadec – LaSalle National Bank

To book Dan for your next corporate event,
call **888-254-1861** or e-mail us at **marketing@danlier.com**

Learn How to "Speak like a Pro"

How would it impact your business if you had the ability to influence and communicate with any audience in any situation? **Dan Lier's High Impact Presentation Training** *(HIPT) course is designed to take any speaker to the next level!*

What you will Learn:
- The Fundamentals of a Powerful Presentation
- The Psychology of Influence
- How to Connect with a Challenging Audience
- Influential Language Patterns
- How to Present with Power
- How to Close with Impact

Limited to 8 participants per course: Available "on-site" or in Las Vegas, NV

"Our entire management team attended and Dan's course and it exceeded all of our expectations. As leaders, all of us needed to improve our speaking and communication skills. Dan trained Tony Robbins' Speakers for years and having access to that type of training was incredible."
Scott Worrell, Regional Sales Manager – Centax Homes

Enroll your team today: **888-254-1861** or **marketing@danlier.com**